Skiing &
Snowboarding

Rosanne Cobb

COLLINS & BROWN

This book is dedicated to Winky, my sports buddy. If there's ever been a girl that needs an instruction manual it's her.

First published in Great Britain in 2005 by
Collins & Brown
The Chrysalis Building
Bramley Road
London W10 6SP

An imprint of **Chrysalis** Books Group plc

1 3 5 7 9 8 6 4 2

British Library Cataloguing-in-Publication Data:
A catalogue record for this book is available from the British Library.

ISBN 1 84340 313 7

Commissioning Editor: Victoria Alers-Hankey
Editor: Fiona Screen
Photographs: Guy Hearn
Design: Simon Daley

Reproduction by Classicscan, Singapore
Printed and bound by CT Printing Ltd, China

The information, advice and exercises set out in this book are only a guide and not intended to cause injury if followed correctly. You should consult your doctor before beginning any fitness regime if you are pregnant or nursing, or if you are elderly or have chronic or recurring medical conditions. The author and publisher disclaim any liability from and in connection with use of the information contained within this book.

Contents

Introduction   6

Chapter 1   Clothing   **14**

Chapter 2   Skis, boards & boots   **24**

Chapter 3   Training & fitness   **52**

Chapter 4   Hitting the slopes   **68**

Chapter 5   Weather & terrain   **98**

Chapter 6   Where to go   **106**

Glossary   **125**

Index   **126**

Acknowledgements   **128**

Introduction

Skiing and snowboarding are two of the most exhilarating sports in the world, and just happen to be fantastic for achieving complete overall fitness. Although it doesn't feel like a training session when you are flying down a mountain, almost all your muscles will be working as you achieve perfect balance and control.

Never be tempted to learn how to ski or snowboard without a qualified instructor unless you're prepared to spend most of your time sampling the delights of the local mountainside hospital. If you follow the guidance of an expert trainer you'll be up and running in no time at all. The instructor will show you, amongst other things, where your weight should be, how to avoid falling over, and how to use a lift. These things are not human nature and so you'll learn far more quickly with an expert to guide you than you would relying on your own trial and error.

Recreational skiing and boarding

There are many distinctions under the generic headings of skiing and snowboarding; competitions now exist in ski jumping, slalom, giant slalom, telemark, Alpine, Nordic, freestyle, freeride, blading, roller-skiing, half-pipe and snowboard cross/skier cross to name only the most well known. However, the standardised sport referred to by the term 'skiing' or 'snowboarding' is the recreational form. This is downhill or 'Alpine' skiing (from its evolution in the Alps) and 'freestyle' or 'freeride' snowboarding.

Alpine skiing differs from other types of skiing in its emphasis on skiing down a hill and catching a lift up, rather than trekking over vast distances of predominantly flat land or jumping huge distances in the air. It is also defined by the equipment used – the skis are shaped with a waist and have fastened-down bindings which prevent heel lift.

Freestyle or freeride snowboarding can be distinguished from other types of snowboarding by the type of boot used. Soft-boot boarding is now standard for beginners. For the more advanced, who are more interested in racing than doing tricks, hard boots can be used. These are almost identical to ski boots.

Nordic skiing also needs a mention as this is a very popular form which doubles as an intense cardio-vascular workout. 'Nordic' is the generic term for the ski disciplines arising out of Norway, such as jumping and cross-country skiing which has now become know as 'cross-country'. Nordic involves travelling over a distance on reasonably flat terrain, where the emphasis is on fitness and endurance. Many resorts identify Nordic trails and some resorts are for cross-country skiing exclusively.

Ski holidays

Unless you are one of the lucky few who live near a snowy mountain, practising the sport of skiing or snowboarding requires serious travel and therefore the sacrifice of at least a few days of your life. This means that skiing and snowboarding usually come wrapped up in a holiday package.

There are as many holiday options as there are types of snowflake, ranging from fully catered and hosted chalets with flights, transfers and ski instructors included, to hostels with beds piled on top of each other where the owners don't care which airport you came from or where you are going to. Each have their merits, but for a beginner or those who like an easy life, the tour operator option is best as you'll get good advice and assistance and will be spoon-fed when you get to your resort.

No-snow options

Although the standard deal for skiing and boarding is a week's holiday or two, it is possible to practise the sport even if you do not live near a mountain. For those in the UK or in other disappointingly low, flat or hot areas, skiing or boarding can be done in artificial snow domes, on grass, or on man-made 'dry slopes'.

Snow domes use artificial snow on an indoor slope and do recreate the feeling of skiing on a mountain for a split second, before you reach the bottom or run into someone on the crowded slope. Although useful for total beginners who want a few lessons, or for freestyle practise on the dedicated sessions where ramps and rails are erected, they are too short for any real progression and can get incredibly icy.

Grass skiing is a sport in its own right. Special skis with wheels are used, and the terrain boards used for grass boarding are big, aggressive skateboards with straps for your feet. This type of skiing is not common and is generally only practised by obsessives who can't bear to have a pause in their ski training over summer.

Dry slopes are generally made from 'Dendex', which is like a big toothbrush carpet, often laid on top of a sprinkler system for lubrication to decrease friction. Dry slope skis and boards are exactly the same as those used for real snow. Although useful for practice, dry slopes are not a satisfactory alternative to the mountains as they are too short and you cannot hope to recreate the feeling of riding on snow. In other words, there is nothing like heading to a snowy resort to ski or board and staying there for the week.

Ski school

A necessary part of learning to ski or board is attending ski school. The term ski school conjures up an image of strict, regimented learning – this is far from the truth; the atmosphere is a relaxed one, with the emphasis placed equally on skill acquisition and having fun, and where even the teachers end up with their faces in the snow. Neither is ski school just for beginners. Even top trainers, who themselves train other instructors, take lessons. If you want to look good on the slopes (having already checked the clothes section of this book), take all the tips on skiing style and boarding on offer. Instructors know the mountain and can always suggest ways of improving your skiing/riding and show you new terrain.

Ski schools exist in practically every skiable area of the world. On bigger hills there will often be a choice of schools, all of which will be fully accredited and insured. Although ski schools are pretty similar in the services they offer, some of the larger ones may include language-specific instructors or limited class numbers.

There are three ways of booking a place at ski school: prior to arrival, either through a tour company or online; in resort on the night of arrival; on the hill in the morning. There shouldn't be any difference in cost so if you are able to book beforehand it will make life slightly less hectic during the inevitable chaos of that first morning. Ski school representatives will visit hotels and chalets in the evening so even if you haven't organised lessons before arrival there is often the opportunity to do it then. Ski schools maintain an obvious presence on the mountain, so you'll be able to find them easily if you don't book until the morning, but get there early in order to make your first lesson on time.

Ski schools offer several different lesson options:

▶ **Daily group lesson** Every ski school will have set group lessons for all abilities. These lessons are the best option for beginners. With an instructor watching you every day, it will stop you getting into bad habits and you'll have the benefit of learning from your peers to help you understand what you may be doing wrong. Groups create a great support set-up. Do not join a group with more than 12 skiers or 8 boarders; unless you have somehow managed to monopolise the instructor's attention, you'll not achieve as much as you could with your time.

▶ **Private group lesson** These are one-off lessons which you organise yourself. Good for intermediates, private group lessons allow you to benefit from practise time on the snow in between lessons and still learn from watching your peers in a group set-up. Regular private group lessons are good for those who feel uncomfortable skiing or boarding with people they don't know, although they can hinder learning if friends are together that are not of the same ability, as the instructor has to gear the lesson to the weakest member of the group.

▶ **Private single lesson** These are good for beginners who need one-to-one support and for the advanced who need concentrated time with an instructor in order to understand how they can improve their already excellent skills.

International variations

Although ski schools are fairly standard across the globe, there are small style variations from country to country in terms of the style of skiing or boarding taught. As a general guide, the Canadians, British, Americans, New Zealanders and Australians are pretty similar in the style of skiing and boarding that they teach. The French, Austrians and other European nations adopt a slightly different style. Both groups think that they are the best and both have merits. The European style has slightly more flair while the English-speaking world is more focused on necessity and the technical aspects of the sport than aesthetics.

How long will it take?

Learning curves differ between snowboarding and skiing. The learning curve for boarding is steep and slightly painful. In the first three days all your effort will be focused on simply staying upright. But by the end of the third day you'll be into your stride (usually). In skiing you will carve out a more sedate route to excellence. Skiers shouldn't spend as much time falling over after the first day but it will take them longer to reach the point where they look as good as a boarder. Either way, after a week of lessons and practise you should be able to navigate confidently around a mountain.

Confidence

Lack of confidence is the main hindrance to learning this sport. Time after time people fall while trying to turn because as they pick up speed they lose confidence and fail to commit to the rest of the turn, so they cannot either go forward to safety or turn back. It sounds trite to say it, but if you fail to believe in yourself you will fail.

Typical day

Unlike most sports, with skiing you learn intensively and your normal life is put completely on hold during that time. The following describes a pretty typical day for a beginner skier or boarder:

7.30   Wake up and wish you were still asleep as the reduced oxygen makes you feel heavier than usual.

8.00   Breakfast of complex carbs with protein and fat to keep you going through the morning.

8.30   Try to get together everything you need for the day. Decide how many layers you need to put on and whether it's a sunglasses or goggles day.

9.00   Make your way to the school meeting-point on the snow.

9.30   Start of lessons. You begin to get your skills back up to the level they were last time you were on snow, whether that was the day before or the previous year.

11.30 Water and snack stop in a mountain restaurant. Sort out any items of clothing that are bugging you, eg socks not pulled up properly, and loosen your boots to give your feet a rest. (It's the hot chocolate, hot wine or coffee time of day. These stimulants aren't recommended, but you're on holiday.)

12.00 Skiing/boarding.

13.30 Light lunch for afternoon energy and lots of water.

14.30 As you will be tiring, your instructor will take it easy for the afternoon session. You'll have some time putting in mileage on the slopes, practising everything you learnt in the morning. If you are skiing without an instructor you will start to feel knackered so should be choosing easy runs.

15.30 Ski school finishes for the day and it's time for another water and snack stop with a light accompaniment of alcohol, sugar or caffeine.

16.00 Leave the mountain and relax for a while in a bar, or head straight home to leave enough time for après-ski activities such as hot-tub bathing, massages or, for the more energetic, ice-skating, bowling or shopping.

19.00 Shower, apply burn lotion to the weird places on your face, ears or neck where you forgot to put on sun cream, and find something to wear that doesn't show how white your arms and body are next to your brown face.

20.00 Dinner. You will be falling asleep as your body musters up all its remaining energy to digest your food.

21.30 Relax and chat about what a good skier/boarder you are now and how some skier/boarder cut you up today and how skiing/boarding is so much better than boarding/skiing and how you will of course do that black run or hit the big kicker tomorrow.

22.30 Time to go out and immerse yourself in the local culture – or the culture of the tour companies operating in the area.

00.00 Hopefully back to your accommodation and into bed.

1.00 Definitely back to your accommodation and into bed.

3.00 Seriously, you are out way too late and will be skiing like a jelly in the morning.

1 Clothing

Skiing and snowboarding demand the correct clothing and
equipment for two reasons. First, the environment is extreme
and very changeable. Second, the sport is a dangerous one
where you and those around you will be travelling at high
speeds. If you think you can make do with inappropriate
clothing and equipment you'll have a sorry experience that
could be dangerous – even fatal. There is a story of a skier
freezing to death on a chair lift that had stopped for some
hours because he was wearing a soaking wet pair of jeans.
It could happen. Besides, you don't want to look like a
novice even if you are one.

Vital basics

Skiing and boarding have some differences in the technical clothing that is required, but the vital basics are the same:

▶ **Dark sunglasses** with a good UV protection rating (close to 100% UVA and UVB screening). Sunblindness is uncomfortable and a very real threat, given that the UV radiation on the slopes is approximately 30% higher than at sea level.

▶ **Goggles** if snowing, or to prevent streaming eyes when going fast.

- ► **Hat** – beanie if cold, sunhat if warm (sunstroke is much more likely on a mountain as you are higher up and the sun is reflected off the white snow, which doubles your exposure).
- ► **Suncream** again, because the white reflective snow doubles your exposure to UV rays.
- ► **Gloves** to protect from 'carpet' burn. Snowboarders need good gloves as boarders touch the snow more often than skiers. Ski gloves don't need to be particularly waterproof. Mittens tend to keep your hands warmer as they allow the air to circulate.
- ► **Helmet** – because skiing and boarding are not called 'extreme sports' merely as a marketing ploy. Helmets are widely worn and are compulsory for under-14s in many countries.

Outerclothing

Jacket

The two main things to remember with your jacket is that quality diminishes with price and that jackets MUST be waterproof. Waterproofing is measured as the hydrostatic water pressure in mm that the material can withstand. A rating of 20,000mm is at the higher end of the range and will cope with most wet conditions you are likely to meet. For serious boarding and skiing at least 5,000mm is recommended. To aid breathability whilst retaining water protection, look for Gore-Tex. This is a polytetrafluoro-ethylene (PTFE) membrane that can be laminated to nylon and polyester fabrics. It stops water but allows breathing, thanks to its construction of microscopic pores which are smaller than water molecules but larger than water vapour. Gore-Tex is also incredibly durable, which helps when you are rolling in trees or carrying sharp-edged skis or boards.

How warm you need your jacket to be really depends on where you are going. Some areas are bitterly cold and your face is likely to get frostbite if uncovered. Other areas can reach beach holiday temperatures at most times of the year. So a good all-round jacket should have a fleece inner jacket which can be removed to leave a waterproof shell for when it is hot. It is better to have a thinner jacket and extra layers underneath than to attempt to adapt a big thick jacket to hot conditions.

A jacket can have all sorts of extras and gimmicks. The most useful features are:

► High zip collar to protect against wind and snow.
► Elasticated sleeves (hidden or visible) to stop snow from getting up your arm.
► Taped zips and seams to ensure total protection from the elements.
► Backing on any zips, especially around the face and neck.

- ▶ Snow skirt to prevent snow from getting down your trousers or up your jacket should you fall.
- ▶ Zipped air vents at the sides for when you heat up but the weather is wet.
- ▶ Outer and inner pockets.
- ▶ Drawstring hood.
- ▶ Chamois or other goggle/glasses cleaning cloth attached to an inner pocket.
- ▶ Detachable inner jacket/fleece.
- ▶ Detachable sleeves for when it is sunny and hot.

Pants

As with jackets, you are looking for waterproofing and breathability. Snowboarders will require highly waterproof pants as, unlike skiers, they have to sit or kneel down every time they stop, so spend a considerable amount of time in the snow. Boarders need a waterproof rating of

5,000mm to 10,000mm as a minimum. Avoid the tendency to get fitted pants; they restrict movement and look pretty bad with your big booted feet and big gloved hands.

The most useful features of pants are:

- ▶ Adjustable waist for when you've eaten too much or want to tuck in extra clothing.
- ▶ Elasticated hems (hidden, preferably).
- ▶ Zipped air vents on the outer or inner thighs to keep you cool.
- ▶ Reinforced knee and bum panels.
- ▶ Extra pockets.

Five tips for keeping warm

1 Keep your head warm with a hat. Most of your body heat disappears through your head.
2 Wear mittens and use some hand warmers (chemical pads that you heat up) in your gloves and boots.
3 Put your arms by your sides with your hands facing out like a penguin and pump your shoulders up and down, keeping your arms straight. This pumps blood to your hands and warms them. The same can be done for your toes if you can find the artery in your thigh that pumps blood to your feet and can pump it with your fingers.
4 Wear a ski mask or scarf around your face if the wind chill is high.
5 Brush excess snow off clothing to keep it dry.

Five tips for keeping cool

1 Keep the sun off your head with a hat or helmet.
2 Choose pants/jacket/gloves with zipped air vents.
3 Wear a high factor suncream to prevent wind and sunburn.
4 Wear a CamelBak to rehydrate yourself every 5–10 minutes.
5 Stay on the shadowed side of the mountain.

Body armour

....

Mainly for snowboarders, as falling is more frequent.

▶ Knee pads. Useful for beginner as well as freestyle boarders. Smaller pads can be worn simply to keep the knees warm when resting on the mountain. Freestyle skiers may wear them but average skiers will fall on their sides, not their knees.
▶ Bum protector. These are shorts with pads to wear under your ski/board pants. They originate from the mountain biking industry and are pretty useful for skiers but more for boarders. Your bum will look big in this but at least it won't be swollen from bruising.
▶ Wrist guards. The most common injury in snowboarding is a fractured wrist. However, opinion is divided as to whether a wrist guard is beneficial. Some believe the guard simply sends the shock further up the arm and can cause a more serious brake.
▶ Back protector. This is useful for extreme riders/skiers or freestylers.
▶ Slalom pads. These are specific to slalom training and you would only buy them if racing.

Key points

....

▶ **To keep safe** wear eye protection, suncream and, ideally, a helmet.
▶ **To keep warm** look for silk or thermals next to the skin with mittens and a beanie/helmet.
▶ **To keep dry** get a technical jacket (as outlined above), pants and gloves.
▶ **To keep cool** wear a hat, and a jacket and pants with air vents.

Underclothing

Your undergarments need to be warm but breathable. This can seem like a contradiction in terms, however 'thermal' materials such as polyester suck moisture away from your body and evaporate it (known as 'wicking'), allowing your body to breath while keeping warm. Look for breathability of around 2,000g (refers to how many grams of moisture can pass through a metre of the material in 24 hours) if you can find the rating, otherwise check the label to see whether it has this wicking capability. Silk is also a natural insulator and is breathable, drawing water away from the skin.

Fleece is a mix of polyester and velour which creates air pockets that trap air and retain body heat. There is no substitute for fleece layers – cotton does not have the same characteristics. Fleece comes in different weights according to how warm it will keep you; 100 weight is a fairly lightweight fleece whereas 300 weight will keep you snuggly warm.

Clothing for optimum warmth

- ▶ Wear thermals such as polyester or silks next to the skin, then fleeces.
- ▶ Layer clothes rather than opting for one big fleece so that you can remove layers when you get hot.
- ▶ Keep your feet warm and comfortable with ski socks – preferably anatomically shaped for extra comfort. Do not be tempted to wear two pairs of normal socks as the fit in your boots will not be as close and your feet will not be so warm. Cold/sore feet are the biggest complaint on the mountain. Don't ruin your day with such a basic mistake as ill-fitting socks.
- ▶ Wear leggings or long johns. You can layer these too!

2 Skis, boards & boots

Ski equipment has developed considerably over the last 50 years and this seems set to continue as growing numbers of skiers and boarders demand higher standards and new materials evolve. Skis and boards are made by layering a combination of bonded materials which give strength and flexibility while being appropriate for different snow conditions. Core materials include wood or polyurethane foam, while the rest of the ski board is made up of monocoque titanium, fibreglass, aluminium, steel, rubber and carbon fibre, amongst other materials. Luckily ski/board manufacturers have a great understanding of how the various materials react together and the impact of temperatures, speed and pressure so you don't have to worry.

Anatomy of a ski

1 Tip
2 Shovel
3 Edge
4 Toe binding
5 Heel binding
6 Brake
7 Tail

Skis for specific uses

- ▶ **Recreational/carving/parabolic** The length of the ski is generally up to the skier's forehead. Carving skis are shaped with a waist to enable easier turning and control.
- ▶ **Freestyle** Shorter and more flexible than carving skis, generally with twin tips to ski switch (ski backwards).
- ▶ **Slalom** Built for speed, longer and narrower with good sidecut for turning.
- ▶ **Powder** Built wider to increase the surface area and spread the weight of the skier so that s/he sits higher on top of deep snow. Bindings are generally placed further back on the ski to keep the tips from sinking into the powder.
- ▶ **Skiercross and freeride** Slightly wider than carving skis to accommodate all terrain including powder, without being too cumbersome on groomed runs.
- ▶ **Nordic/telemark** The ski is like a carving ski but softer, with bindings which hold only the toe firm, allowing the heel to lift for walking.
- ▶ **Langlauf/cross-country** Built for the flats, very thin and light.
- ▶ **Ski mountaineering/ski touring** Off-piste downhill skis with a telemark-type binding which locks firmly into place for descending the mountain.
- ▶ **Ski jumping** Long, wide skis built to fly, these are shaped to create a cushion of air underneath the jumper.

How to choose recreational skis

Length

Ever since the introduction of 'carving' skis (also known as 'parabolic' skis), which are shaped so that the tips and shovel are wider than the waist, it is now universally acknowledged that a shorter ski is a more useful ski. However, there are still variations, which relate to your ability. Beginner recreational skiers should aim for skis that reach between the shoulder and the forehead, preferably somewhere around the nose, intermediates around head height and advanced up to 20cm above the head. If skis are for a lighter person they should be shorter, whilst heavier skiers should choose slightly longer ones. Generally longer skis are good for going fast and shorter skis better for freestyle or the bumps (see page 92), meaning that even advanced skiers have a choice of longer or shorter skis, depending on the activity.

Shape

The shape of a ski differs according to the type of snow and the type of skiing. The factors which influence a ski's performance are the sidecut and the width difference between the shovel and tail (the taper angle). Nearly all downhill skis are carving or parabolic. This enables easier turning, smaller radius turns and carving. The most important consideration in choosing a downhill ski is how 'waisted' it is. A pronounced sidecut with a very thin waist is great for very quick turns but may be too aggressive for an intermediate skier. A wide waist with little sidecut will make turning more difficult. Look for a middle-of-the-road ski where the waist is slightly thinner than your boot and where the sidecut is obvious.

Edges

The 'effective' edge of a ski is the amount of the edge that grips the snow. This is usually related to (although is not the same as) the length of the ski and shortening or lengthening this edge has the same effects as does shortening or lengthening the ski (see above).

Camber

The camber evenly distributes the pressure of the skier across the length of the ski. Simply put, it is how flexible the ski is. The camber enables the ski to absorb bumps and helps it 'pop' out of turns or jumps. How much camber your skis need is related to your weight. Check the weight specifications that the manufacturer gives for the ski. The heavier you are, the more camber you need in your ski. However, your development as a skier is also a factor; as you advance and become more aggressive, you can use stiffer skis as you will be applying more pressure at higher speeds. A stiffer ski will also give you stability at high speeds.

Other factors

The weight of a ski can be unevenly distributed to make it more or less stable at higher speeds in a straight line, or to make it easier or more difficult to turn. If more weight is placed at the tip and tail of the ski, it will be more stable at high speeds but harder to turn. This is referred to as 'swing weight'.

The rigidity of a ski in terms of twisting is also a factor influencing performance. When a ski is torsionally rigid, it is more responsive to pressure. A ski with more torsional flex will be more forgiving.

How to choose ski boots

Boots are so important yet are often last on the list when buying new equipment. Without well-fitting boots, the best skis in the world will perform like planks of wood and you will have a miserable experience.

Boots are made of a tough plastic outer shell and a soft inner boot. The most important factor in choosing a boot is that it fits tightly all

around the foot and leg without being tighter or looser in any one place or creating pressure points. Boots are not completely rigid; they flex around the ankle to enable you to bend your knees. This gives you the 'forward lean' necessary for skiing, forcing you to bend your knees slightly but not excessively (unless you are considering racing).

The flex of a boot needs to be supportive without being too stiff or giving a sudden halt. Much like the binding release setting (see below), the flex of a boot is related to the height, weight and ability of the skier as well as to what kind of skiing the boot will be used for. If your boot is not fitting as it should and your foot 'swims around', is too tight or has sore points due to extra pressure, you can experiment with custom-moulded footbeds or extra padding. You might even try taking a knife to points of the outer shell in order to achieve a better fit.

How to choose ski bindings

Bindings hold the boot as tight as possible to the ski. They are spring-loaded and flexible to allow for varying pressure and varying skiing movement, and to enable your boot to pop out if needed. Bindings can be screwed to your ski or attached to a binding plate. Plates are generally recommended as they eliminate the 'dead spot' created when bindings are fixed directly to the ski and they achieve more grip on turns by adding height, and more flex as they require minimal attachment points of the ski. Bindings are attached in the middle of the waist of the ski and are adjustable to suit the individual.

To correctly set bindings to hold a boot, a binding release setting (or 'DIN' – Deutsche Industrie Normen – setting) is used. The binding release setting relates to how tight your bindings must be to ensure that you stay in them while skiing but come out of them if you fall. If the setting is

Setting release values

These values err on the side of caution. As you progress you will want a higher setting so that your skis stay on even when you apply extreme pressure.

Data about the skier			Pre-set value z depends on the boot sole length in mm						Test data	
Skier weight kg	Skier height cm	Code for skier	<250	251 – 270	271 – 290	291 – 310	311 – 330	>331	Twist MZ NM	Front fall MY NM
									5	18
10–13		A	0.75	0.75					8	29
14–17		B	1	1	0.75				11	40
18–21		C	1.5	1.25	1				14	52
22–25		D	1.75	1.5	1.5	1.25			17	64
26–30		E	2.25	2	1.75	1.5	1.5		20	75
31–35		F	2.75	2.5	2.25	2	1.75	1.75	23	87
36–41		G	3.5	3	2.75	2.5	2.25	2	27	102
42–48	<148	H		3.5	3	3	2.75	2.5	31	120
49–57	149–157	I		4.5	4	3.5	3.5	3	37	141
58–66	158–166	J		5.5	5	4.5	4	3.5	43	165
67–78	167–178	K		6.5	6	5.5	5	4.5	50	194
78–94	179–194	L		7.5	7	6.5	6	5.5	58	229
>95	>195	M			8.5	8	7	6.5	67	271
		N			10	9.5	8.5	8	78	320
		O			11.5	11	10	9.5	91	380
		P							105	452
										540

correct, your ski will come off in a fall to minimize injury, but won't pop off every time you catch an edge or put pressure on it. The setting is determined based on five factors: ability, height, weight, age and boot sole length. Use the chart opposite but always check the manufacturer's own guide as the numerical settings can vary.

When buying bindings, ideally look for those where your own setting is somewhere in the middle of the range the binding offers. You should also make sure that, in relation to your boots, a) the toe binding is not sitting too low (the toe of your boot will be pinched); b) the toe binding is not too wide (there will be side to side movement); or c) the binding is too narrow (there will be undue pressure on your boot).

How to choose poles

Poles are lightweight, usually made of graphite, aluminium or composite materials. Graphite is the toughest lightweight, whereas aluminium is more likely to snap under pressure. Unless you are racing, poles are straight and with standardised features: a tip, basket, shaft and handle. The only technical consideration when buying a pole for recreational downhill skiing is your height. As a general guide to length, turn the pole upside down and hold it just under the basket. Maintain a flexed ski position, with the pole placed slightly in front of you. In this position, your elbow should be at a right angle as the pole rests on the ground, and your forearm should be parallel to the ground. Getting the length of your poles right is important, as too short or long a pole will affect your basic stance and therefore your overall stability.

How to handle your boots, skis and poles

Boots

Open the boots right up to avoid ankle injury when you are putting them on. Don't shove your feet in as if you are trying to get toothpaste back in the tube. Leave the buckles undone or loose to walk in (unless they have a 'walk mode', where a flick of a switch makes them more flexible). When you get to the top of a run, do the buckles up as tight as you can without cutting off the blood supply. Start with the middle buckle to pull your ankle back to the right position. Then work up or down, and return to the middle again if you need to repeat. When you are skiing you should not feel your heels lift when flexing your knees. If you do, your boots do not fit properly and you are losing a degree of control.

Skis

Make sure your ski is flat and, if on a slope, put the ski across the fall line. If the slope is steep you will have to dig the uphill edge into the snow to get the ski flat for you to put it on. Make sure there are no lumps of snow in the binding mechanism or on the bottom of your boot. If there is residual snow, use your pole to dig it out – or you can kick the top of the binding and scrape the snow off the sole of your boot.

The binding has only two positions; open and shut. It must be open to put your foot in, meaning the heel lever is in the 'down' position. Push your toe firmly into the toe binding and stamp the heel down into the heel binding so that it snaps shut.

Poles

Put your hand all the way through the strap and hold both the grip and the strap. This will allow you to have more control if for any reason you let go of your pole.

Anatomy of a snowboard

1 Bindings
2 High back
3 Tail
4 Stomp pad
5 Toe edge
6 Heel edge
7 Nose

Boards for specific uses

- ▶ **Freestyle** Twin tipped, flexible and shorter for quick turns, easy rotations and riding switch.
- ▶ **Freeride** Twin tipped but directional and stiffer for all-round snow conditions and freestyle.
- ▶ **Slalom/carve** Directional narrow boards, ridden with hard boots for speed and responsiveness.

How to choose a board

These days boards tend to be judged on their graphics or the signature on them rather than their technical qualities. However, boards are just as technical as skis and many of the same factors influence their performance. Their construction is also much the same as skis, with fibreglass, polyethylene and wood among the common materials. Although every board manufacturer is different, the following guidelines count for all types when buying or hiring a board for recreational snowboarding:

Length

The length of the board you should go for depends mainly on your height, but your weight, ability and what you are using it for should also be taken into account. The board can reach anywhere between your shoulder and your forehead, ideally to your chin for a beginner, nose for intermediate and forehead for advanced. Freestyle boards are shorter, to enable easier jibbing, whilst slalom boards are longer for stability at higher speeds.

Shape

There are three different board shapes – directional (carve/slalom), directional twin tip (freeride) and twin tip (freestyle).

- ▶ **Directional** boards are much like a big ski, with a raised tip and flat tail. The same factors affect their performance as for skis (see above).
- ▶ **Directional twin tip** boards are weighted and shaped asymmetrically as the rider mainly rides in one direction but can also ride fakie (backwards/switch), with the tail lifted from the snow as the nose is.
- ▶ **Twin tip (freestyle)** boards are symmetrical in shape and flex pattern so that they can be ridden both ways.

Just like skis, boards are shaped with a sidecut to assist turning and carving. Whereas freestyle boards are symmetrical on both the horizontal and vertical axes, freeride boards have a progressive sidecut which means that although they are symmetrical if folded along the length of the board, they are asymmetrical if folded horizontally – the greater radius at the nose allows easier turn initiation while the tighter radius at the tail powers the board out of each turn by forcing it to turn more tightly.

The sidecut of the board determines the radius of carved turns, so the more sidecut, the shorter the turn. Although you would always look for a board with good sidecut for recreational snowboarding, a beginner would find a very shaped board difficult to manage.

The width of the waist of the board influences how quickly you can change edges and thus how fast you can make your turns. Unlike with skis however, the waist width is also relevant to the size of your feet, as your feet sit across the width of the board. Slalom boards can be much thinner as the feet are placed almost facing forwards, one behind the other.

Edges

These steel strips along the edge of a board are pretty standard. The 'effective' edge of a board is the amount of the edge that grips the snow. A longer effective edge means more grip but makes it harder to turn, so a beginner would choose a board with less effective edge just the same as they would choose a shorter board. A slalom board will have a toe side effective edge starting higher up the board than the heel side to compensate for the fact that the toes are pressuring higher up the board than the heels.

Camber

Camber gives the board its 'pop', which is felt in turns and in jibbing, exactly the same as the camber in a ski (see page 31). A 'dead' board with little or no camber will be slower to respond.

Other factors

Just as with skis, swing weight and torsional flex will help determine your choice. Your stability increases with greater swing weight (with more weight at the nose and tail) and decreases with diminished swing weight (more weight closer to the centre of the board).

Torsional rigidity will make your board more stable at higher speeds, and give greater responsiveness when turning and applying pressure to the board. Greater torsional flex makes turn initiation easier and gives a more forgiving ride.

The 'stomp pad' is a rough area in between the bindings. This is where you can place your back foot when it is not strapped into the bindings to stop it slipping off the smooth topsheet of your board. The stomp pad need not be a factor when you are buying a board, as you stick it on afterwards, but is an integral part of your board set-up.

How to choose snowboard boots

Snowboard boots are one area in which boarding triumphs over skiing. Recreational snowboard boots are soft and your knees don't have to bend both ways simply to allow you to look normal when walking in them. However, boots are getting stiffer to offer better responsiveness from your board as well as support to prevent unnecessary injury. When choosing boots make sure you have no heel lift when they are laced up, and go for the stiffest boots you can while still being able to flex. If buying new, make

sure your boots are a little too tight, as they will give after a few weeks' wear. The more advanced and/or heavy you are, the stiffer your boots can be. However, if you are intending on mainly freestyle boarding, choose a boot with more flex. If speed is your goal, choose a stiff boot. Whichever boot you choose, make sure it has forward lean so that when it is laced up you are forced to bend at the knee when your foot is flat on the ground.

▶ **Step-in boots** are made specifically for step-in bindings and are more rigid than other boots. They cannot be used with other types of bindings. Make sure they are sufficiently supportive and that your foot is unable to move forwards, backwards or from side to side. Any movement will reduce your control and the responsiveness of the board and can cause unnecessary injury.

▶ **Hard boots** are used for carve boards in disciplines such as slalom, giant slalom and snowboard cross. These can be ski boots or a ski-boot hybrid which flex medially as well laterally to account for the different movements in boarding.

How to choose snowboard bindings

There are three types of snowboard binding: – standard, step-in and plate.

▶ **Standard** bindings are the most commonly used in recreational riding. They consist of a base plate, a high back and usually two straps. A higher back gives greater support, and more forward lean on the high back allows a more aggressive ride (high backs usually have adjustable forward lean).

► **Step-in bindings** are for soft boots and are popular with beginners who are endlessly putting on and taking off their boards and do not want to spend ages fiddling about with annoying straps. These bindings have a base plate and occasionally a high back to give additional support. The downsides of step-in bindings are that they fit only one type of boot and are not easy to use when on a steep slope or in deep snow.

► **Plate bindings** are used with hard boots and are not generally suitable for beginners or for recreational riding. This type of binding has a base plate and a toe and heel fastening which the hard boots clip into.

Binding set-up

Binding set-up is often completely misunderstood but is in fact relatively straightforward. Most recreational bindings will have three or four screws holding down the base plate, or some other type of adjustable fastening.

► Place the bindings shoulder-width apart (or to be more technical, a distance equal to 30% of your height), or a little wider for freestyle to reduce the swing weight.

► Place the bindings in the middle of the waist of the board or slightly nearer the tail if riding powder or freeriding.

► The angle of your bindings for recreational riding should relate to the way your knees bend, in order to prevent unnecessary strain. The angle should be at around 30° for your right foot and -30° for your left, where zero is on a line perpendicular to the length of the board.

► For carve boards both feet will be angled in the same direction, set slightly back on the board and will be a little closer together than for recreational riding.

How to put on boots and bindings

Boots

Whether they are laced or buckled, you should do up your boots tightly so that you cannot fit your finger in between the straps/laces and boot. A common mistake is leaving boots too loose and doing up the bindings to compensate, resulting in aching, cramping and cold feet. Tighten as much as possible without cutting off the blood, and tighten again every time you stop for a break.

Bindings

By the time you are on the mountain you should have decided whether you are goofy or regular and have set up your bindings accordingly. It doesn't really matter which foot you decide to put at the front as in the end you will be riding with both feet forward (not at the same time; unless you're a pork pie short of a picnic). However, if you have experience of any other related sports such as windsurfing, skating or surfing, then it's advisable to choose the foot that you put forward for these. If you're not sure which one to choose, get someone to push you from behind when you are stationary and unaware. Whichever foot you fall on to should be your front foot.

Once you have chosen whether you are goofy or regular, STICK to it. Beginners have a tendency to think they have chosen the wrong foot by the second day, as they spend more time going backwards than forwards. This has nothing to do with being goofy or regular; it is because fear forces their weight on the back foot, which makes them go backwards. In any case, it doesn't matter if your board is set up with the wrong foot

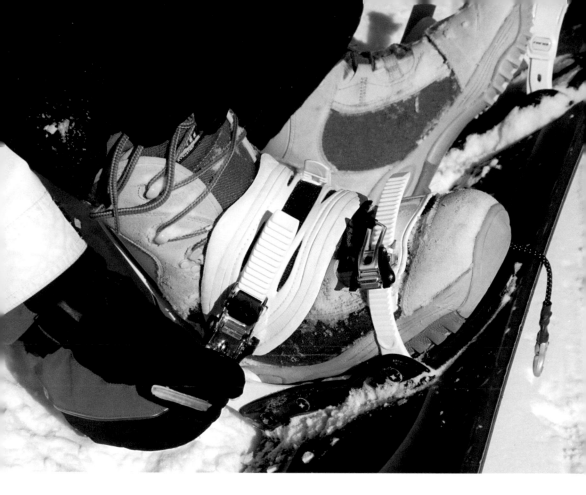

forward for a day as initially you will be side slipping (see page 82) equally right and left.

Putting on bindings is often done on a slope rather than the flat, which makes it all the more tricky, as boards do not have brakes like skis; if you let go, the board will disappear and can do serious damage in its bid for freedom. It is generally easier to put your board on while sitting down, especially on a slope. Put the leash on first if there is one, around your front foot. For bindings with straps, put your front foot in first and do up the ankle binding to pull the foot to the back of the binding. Then do up the toe strap. Repeat for the back foot, either sitting down or standing. For step-in bindings, make sure there is no snow on the base plate, do up the leash if there is one, put in your front foot first with the board as flat as you can make it, then your back foot.

Hiring versus buying

Your decision whether to hire or buy your equipment is dependent on the following: price, comfort and performance, fashion, and your own development as a skier or boarder.

► **Price** Generally speaking, it will work out cheaper to buy your own equipment if you intend to spend more than a couple of weeks per year on the slopes. However, hiring means you do not have any maintenance costs; you can give your equipment back at the end of your trip without worrying about waxing, or how many holes you've gouged out of the bottom. And you won't incur any transport costs.

► **Comfort and performance** Generally, your own equipement will both fit you better and be better looked after, meaning it is likely to be more comfortable and improve your performance. Hire boots will have moulded to a hundred feet before yours and hire skis or boards may be at the end of their life. However, you can always pay a bit extra for the latest models when hiring equipment.

► **Fashion** If you have the money to spend, that's fine, but don't spend money on bling skis or labelled-up boards before you buy your boots, as boots are the most important part of your equipment. You can still hire the latest equipment but your choice is more limited and of course you cannot customise. If you do not ski often, hiring allows you to keep up with the latest technology.

► **Your development** Equipment varies hugely from brand to brand and model to model. As you progress you will find you like one particular pair of skis or board. This is a problem of hiring as you'll be changing frequently to equipment that does not perform as yours does and this will hinder your development.

Hire if you are a once-in-while skier/boarder as it is cheaper. Buy if you go more regularly or are of a high standard.

Second-hand equipment

If you are buying skis or a board second hand make sure it still has some camber. Also ensure that the board or skis are not delaminated anywhere, as this will allow water to reach the core (in other words, check there are no deep holes or discolouring along the edges). Small surface imperfections can be fixed easily and cheaply as long they are not touching the edges of the board, although 'bubbling' on the base or shape imperfections cannot. Make sure the ski or board still has sufficient base left and has not been ground so much that it is practically bare.

As for second-hand poles, as long as they are the right height and as light as you can get them, they should be fine.

NEVER buy boots second hand. They are the most important piece of equipment and they need to fit your feet, not someone else's. Boots get looser and less waterproof over time, both of which will hinder your enjoyment and progress.

Note If you choose to hire, you can often fit and order skis before you leave your home country which will be available for your arrival in resort. Hire skis will be parabolic and hire boards will be twin tip with soft-boot bindings unless you request anything different.

If you do choose to buy, don't forget to pick up a board/ski bag and a boot bag in which to transport your equipment. It keeps them in better condition and, in any case, airlines often won't take them as luggage unless they are wrapped up or bagged in some way. Be aware that cheapo airlines will make you pay extra for weighing down their planes with your gear.

Tips on how to carry skis and boards

Carrying your equipment in the correct way is an essential lesson to learn if you want to progress past the 'novice', ungainly stage of skiing. Something as simple as placing your skis too far up your shoulder will give you away as someone who knows as much about skiing as the average ski instructor knows about higher maths.

Skis and poles

Put the poles together in one hand. Then put the skis together so that the brakes 'lock' onto each other. Having checked that there is no one standing too near you, swing your skis onto one shoulder so that the bindings sit just behind it. This will give enough weight behind your shoulder to enable you to keep your skis still by balancing the pressure with your arm resting on the front of the skis. If you are in a queue, this method is obviously going to cause problems so carry the skis together in an upright position by hooking your hand under the bindings. Keep your poles together in a similar upright position and watch behind you as you enthusiastically describe your last 10-foot jump that no-one saw, unless you want the end of your pole to take someone's eye out.

Board

A board is slightly easier to carry than skis and presents less of a hazard to others. But carrying it on your shoulder or on your back just doesn't look good. The easiest way to carry your board is with one hand placed in between the bindings and with the bindings facing away from you. This means the board naturally rests against your arm instead of your body. When you put your board down make sure you place it binding side to the snow, as it has no brakes and will disappear if someone nudges it when you are on a slope.

Maintenance for skis and boards

Boards and skis will dry out and become damaged if not cared for properly. Maintenance is not complicated and will give your equipment a good long life. Good board and ski maintenance consists of waxing, edging, base repairs and base grinding. Ideally get a professional to show you how to wax and maintain your equipment. Damage can be caused if you don't know what you are doing.

Waxing

Ideally you should wax your board/skis every day, even with the newer base materials such as polyethylene plastic. In reality, the best most of us can manage is to wax once a fortnight; weekly if the snow is wet. If you know your board is going to lie idle for several months, put loads of wax on and leave it, scraping it just before you next use it.

There are three types of waxing of which hot waxing is the best and spray or rub-on waxing are just used now and then for convenience. Hot waxing seals the base by warming it so that the fibres stand up and the pores open, then the wax seeps in and solidifies.

▶ First clean the base with a clean cloth and a solvent and dry it well (otherwise the wax will not be absorbed properly). If there are any significant gouges, P-Tex (a type of plastic readily available in any ski shop) them as described below.

▶ Choose a wax appropriate for the snow and air temperatures (there will be a guide on the packaging), or a universal wax if you don't know the conditions, and melt the wax with an iron onto the base of the ski or board. Make sure the iron is not too hot otherwise it will blister the base. (You can tell if it is too hot by how quickly the wax melts on the iron. If the wax drips in a steady stream it is too hot; you're looking for a couple of drips per second, which usually means the iron is set to around 115˚).

▶ Iron the wax on the ski/board, making sure to keep the iron moving. When the wax stays melted all over the base (and usually the camber is reversed, so the ski/board lies more flat), the ski/board is at optimum temperature to absorb the wax.

▶ Leave it ideally for 8 hours.

▶ Scrape the wax off the base with a smooth plastic scraper. Use even strokes. Make sure this is done at an angle, or you will rip out the wax and cause damage to the fibres.

▶ Finish by lightly buffing the base of the ski/board with a nylon brush. This prevents it from being too smooth, which can cause a suction effect on the snow and slow you down.

Edging

Taking out little nicks as well as sharpening your edges improves your board or ski's grip on the snow. However, edges that are too sharp will catch on the snow so in reality edging badly is pretty much the same as not edging at all. Edge your skis/board every day if it is icy, otherwise do it every week.

The edge has two surfaces which join approximately at a right angle – the base edge and the sidewall edge. Start by smoothing any nicks or hardened areas on the edges with emery paper or a deburring stone.

- ▶ Starting on the sidewall edge, run a file (the right way around!) the length of the board 3 or 4 times until the surface is smooth.
- ▶ Repeat for the base edge. There is a finite amount of metal so do not sharpen the edges beyond what is necessary.
- ▶ Detune the edge so that it is not too sharp by setting the guide of the file to one degree and running it along the length of the edge. The edges also need to be dulled at the tip and tail at the point where the edge touches the snow, otherwise the ski or board will catch on turns or turn too quickly.

Base repairs

If you have any significant nicks or gouges, you need to fill them with P-Tex on the same day they occur:

- ▶ Melt a piece of P-Tex until it burns with a blue rather than yellow flame (alternatively use a piece of plastic – the stuff that holds together six packs of beer will do).
- ▶ Drip the molten P-Tex into the hole (it must be clean – use a solvent and cloth) until it is filled.
- ▶ Leave it to cool and then scrape of any surplus
- ▶ Finally, use emery paper until the surface is smooth.

Base grinding

This is like a facelift for the base and should be carried out by a professional about once every 10 weeks of skiing. Base grinding removes a layer of the base to restore it to optimum condition, so go carefully as there's only so much base.

3 Training & fitness

Although skiing is generally practiced while on holiday, you shouldn't consider it merely a holiday activity – it is a demanding sport. Unless you do 7 hours of physical activity per day as part of your normal routine, then during your skiing holiday you will be significantly increasing your level of exercise, which will place strain on your body. In addition, the air is thinner at altitude so any exercise is more difficult and demands greater effort. So, if your body is used to little more than the occasional run for a bus, you need to gear yourself up for the abuse that skiing can inflict upon it and put in some good preparation before you hit the snow. Exercising with ski-specific exercises as well as working on general cardiac routines are intelligent ways to prepare.

Fitness programme

The following fitness programme is useful as a general guide only. Individual strengths and weaknesses should be assessed by a doctor, especially if you are over 35. If you have any diseases or a heart condition, high blood pressure, difficulty with breathing or bone, muscle, ligament or tendon problems – or if you are overweight or inactive – chat to your doctor about the risk of skiing. If you are healthy and relatively active, a fitness professional can assess you and take into account any weaknesses when planning a programme for you. This will help avoid any potential injuries.

Example exercises described below are chosen because they involve similar motions and movements to those of skiing and boarding and so will build up the strength and endurance of the appropriate muscles, as well as increasing cardio-respiratory endurance. Together these and flexibility make up your general level of fitness. Ideally you should aim to vary your fitness schedule.

Cardiovascular fitness

2 months prior to skiing
NB include a 5–10 minute warm-up and warm-down period either side of each exercise session. The warm-up/warm-down should consist of low-level exercise (walking/jogging/arm rotations) and stretching movements.
▶ 1-hour swim per week (increases overall endurance and provides good muscle workout).
▶ 1-hour bike ride/rollerblade per week (increases leg strength and endurance).
▶ 1 hour of rowing per week (increases cardiovascular fitness and strengthens arms, legs and trunk muscles).

1 month prior to skiing

5–10 min warm-up and warm-down either side of each exercise session.

▶ 1½-hour swim per week.

▶ 1½-hour bike ride/rollerblade per week.

▶ 1½ hours rowing per week.

If possible include a few hours per week skiing/boarding on a local slope.

Try not to exhaust your muscles' supply of glycogen, ATP (adenosine triphosphate) and CP (creatine phosphate) by hard exercise in the few days before you start your trip.

Stretches for flexibility, strength and endurance

In addition to the exercise routine outlined on pages 54–55, short but targeted sessions to increase flexibility, as well as the strength and endurance of specific muscle groups are a great idea. These exercises can also be used on your ski trip as part of your warm up/cool down routine. Do not stretch before you have warmed up your body with some aerobic activity; if you stretch a cold elastic band, it snaps

Muscular endurance and strength training are similar exercises but with different aims. Strength training improves muscle size to cope with greater loads whereas endurance training doesn't actually increase the muscle size but impoves the ability of muscle groups to make repetitive movements. An example of some flexibilty, strength and endurance exercises are below:

1   **Quadricep (front of thigh) stretch for flexibility** Holding on to a stationary object if needed for balance, stand on one foot. Keep one leg straight and lift the other foot behind you, grasping it with your free hand. Push your hips forward and your bent knee back so that your thigh is in line with your other leg. Hold this position for 30 seconds, then rest. Repeat on the other side.

2   **Calf stretch for flexibility** Stand with one foot in front of the other with your front leg bent and your back leg straight. With both feet flat on the floor and keeping both feet pointing forwards, push on your

back leg and lower your hips. Hold this position for 30 seconds, then rest. Repeat 4 times before changing legs.

3 **Groin stretch for flexibility** Sit with your back straight, or lie on your back, with the soles of your feet together and slowly relax letting your knees drop until it is slightly uncomfortable. Hold this position for 30 seconds before bringing your knees back up. Repeat 4 times.

4 **Squats for strength and endurance** Stand with your feet shoulder-width apart. Keeping both of your feet flat on the floor and your back straight, lower your centre of gravity by flexing at the knees and hips. When your thighs are parallel with the floor push back up again to a standing position. Repeat 10 times. Rest and repeat 4 times. To build endurance, increase the amount of repetitions. To build strength do the exercise with a barbell across the back of your shoulders, or using only one foot at at time.

5 **The plank for stength and endurance** From a lying down position on a firm surface, raise yourself up on to your forearms and your toes. Make sure your back and legs are straight, much like a press-up. Do not lower or raise your bottom. Hold this position for 10 seconds. Rest and repeat 4 times. As you become used to this position, increase the length of time you hold it, and/or how many times you repeat the exercise.

On the ski trip

Before your day begins It's important to do an appropriate warm-up
prior to going on your first run. The warm-up is two-fold, with a first phase
to get the blood circulating and a second phase to stretch specific muscle
groups. A brisk walk to the cable car in the morning, some jogging on the
spot or some squats and lunges will get the blood circulating. For the
stretching, concentrate on the following key muscles (but do not allow
yourself to get cold or your 'warm-up' becomes self-defeating): quads,
hams and gluts, upper limbs. If in doubt, stretch by mimicking the
movements you make when you ski or ride, as these will be the muscles
that need stretching. Boarders should pay extra attention to their inner
thigh muscles (adductors), neck muscles (flexors and extensors) and inner
arm muscles (wrist flexors), as these tend to get a hammering. Any

muscles you feel are sore on your second morning are the ones to concentrate on in the future.

During your day When you break for lunch or a drink, your muscles start to seize up. So walk around for a minute if you are stopping for more than 20 minutes, and stretch gently with a short walk before setting off again.

After your day finishes When you've completed your last run of the day, stretch your muscles again and have a gentle walk around before sitting down to relax. Ideally stretch after a warm shower in the evening or, if you are lucky enough to be staying somewhere that has a pool, go for swim. Take a shower and switch between hot and cold. This can reduce inflammation of exercised muscles, minimising build-up of lactic acid, which leads to sore, stiff muscles.

Nutrition

Eating poorly will severely impact on your enjoyment of any day on the slopes. Too much or too little food before exercising are both detrimental. Eating immediately before exercise will slow you down and may make you feel sluggish. This is because your muscles and digestive system are competing for energy. But don't be tempted to skip any meal, as low blood sugar may make you weak and dizzy, and hamper your co-ordination.

► **Carbohydrate** is the body's main source of fuel and is vital for activities such as skiing. Any excess carbohydrate in the body is stored as glycogen, which is what the muscles use for energy. Therefore, although you should always eat a balanced diet to absorb all the nutrients your body needs, special attention should be given to your carbohydrate intake when skiing. Avoid high-fibre carbohydrates like beans, lentils and some fruits immediately before exercise, as these may cause cramps or diarrhoea.
► **Fats** are not the best source of energy, but your body needs them nonetheless. A high intake of fat just prior to exercise will sit uncomfortably in your stomach so try to impose some limits and time your intake sensibly.
► **Proteins** are needed to help your muscles repair after exercise.
► **Water** is essential to any exercise routine. During intense activity try to drink water every 20 minutes, and at least 8 glasses on any one day. As a rule of thumb, 1 litre of water should be taken for every hour of activity. When exercise is taken over a prolonged period of time it is not easy to maintain the balance needed to keep you from dehydrating. So sports drinks, which rehydrate you more quickly than water and maintain your electrolyte balance, are therefore a good alternative.

What to eat when

The following is a general guideline. Everyone has different needs however, so consult a nutritionist to find what is best for you.

Breakfast*
- Lots of carbohydrates such as cereals, bread and fruit for energy
- Some protein and fat to slow down the absorption of sugar
- At least one glass of water – not diuretics like tea or coffee

Mid-morning snack
- Carbohydrates such as fruit or bread to keep up your energy. If there is no other choice, eating chocolate or drinking a fizzy drink as a short-term sugar boost is better than not eating at all when you need energy
- Water

Lunch
Again, you don't need a large meal, but don't skip lunch either – you'll need the energy.
- Carbohydrates such as pasta, vegetables
- Some proteins and fats such as meats and nuts
- Water

Afternoon snack
Keep up your energy through the afternoon with:
- Carboyhdrates
- Water

Dinner
Although not always practical, try to eat a balanced evening meal soon after you stop skiing as this will help your muscles recover.
- Carbohydrates such as vegetables, pasta and rice
- Protein such as fish, meat, beans and lentils
- Fats such as nuts, oily fish or oils

*NB: Eat as early as possible. If you have to eat immediately before skiing (within an hour), eat a smaller breakfast

Injuries

Happily, the number of injuries on ski slopes is falling, but there are still some firm favourites which mountainside clinics are frequently called to attend to. Most are short-lived and can be forgotten about within a matter of weeks, if not days. A small percentage are serious. Here are the typical ski- or board-related injuries, with advice on how to treat them. This advice should not be seen as a replacement for a visit to the doctor. To be safe, always seek medical attention if you feel you may have any of the symptoms below.

Concussion

Head injuries are a problem for snowboarders, because of the way boarders fall. While skiers fall sideways, boarders tend to fall backwards, slamming the head onto the ground. Concussion occurs when the head is hit hard and often (but not always) results in unconsciousness. The concussed person may feel sick, dizzy, have blurred vision, memory loss and convulsions. If one pupil is larger than the other, or the person goes numb, falls asleep and cannot be wakened, the concussion is serious.
Treatment Anyone with concussion should see a doctor who may do a brain scan to check for bleeding or other damage. Slight concussion needs monitoring as symptoms can continue for weeks, although if there is no other injury to the brain, the concussion will subside without the need for medical intervention. Young people should be careful to avoid any further head injuries for the 3 months following unconsciousness – the young are more at risk of brain damage from further knocks during this period.

Pulled neck/whiplash

More common for snowboarders who fall back on their bums than for skiers who fall sideways, the neck injury is a pretty everyday occurrence.

Luckily, whiplash it is not often a serious injury, more just a major pain in the neck.

Treatment Although total prevention is unrealistic, you will reduce your risk by warming up your neck before riding and making sure your circulation is good before jumping or attempting any manoeuvres that carry the risk of a fall. Ice for the first 24–48 hours and then take time for a massage. When all the swelling and bruising has gone, apply heat.

Fractures

Fractures can occur on any bone in the body, but are more common on the wrist, collar bone, rib or lower leg. Fractures can be simple, compound, or if you are really unlucky, comminuted (where there are three or more bone fragments). You can often spot a fracture by a bulge or lump under the skin (or a bone sticking out!).

Treatment All fractures need to be kept still to let the bone set. Depending on the severity of the break, some may need surgery and may take months to heal with splints pins or braces to immobilise the bone, while others may require only a simple cast for a couple of weeks.

Pulled thumb ligament

'Skier's thumb' is a ligament injury which occurs at the base of the thumb and is usually the result of fall when your outstretched hand hits the ground while still holding the pole. This causes the thumb to hyper-extend, damaging the ligament. However, it sometimes happens to boarders on a dry slope too, when the thumb gets caught in the matting ... and it really really hurts.

Treatment Initially rest and ice the thumb. A doctor will tape the thumb in a comfortable position that allows the damaged ligament to rest. Depending on how severe the injury is, you may require physiotherapy for strength and mobility, or possibly immediate surgery if the ligament is ripped. However, you may be able to carry on skiing, as long as you take care to wrap the pole strap around your wrist and not just your hand.

Achilles tendon rupture

Your Achilles is used every time you push off from your toes or point them forward, so is particularly at risk when skiing and boarding. If you feel a persistent pain at the back of your heel or lower leg, you may have simply stretched your tendon rather than ruptured it. Resting will heal it. Always see your doctor, as even a small tear can cause rupture if untreated.

Treatment You can treat the injury with rest and by wearing a restrictive garment, but the chance of the tendon reattaching itself is greatly improved with surgery.

Bruising

Bruising isn't particularly life-threatening but can mask underlying problems so get your bruises checked out. A bruised coccyx is one of the most common boarders' ailments and can last for months, unfortunately, whereas skiers tend to suffer a random selection of equipment-induced bruises.

Treatment Arnica is fantastic, although being a homeopathic remedy it remains largely untested. Otherwise an anti-inflammatory drug, coupled with sitting it out for a week or two, should do the trick.

Altitude sickness

Some ski resorts are located above 3,000m/10,000ft. At such heights, the reduced oxygen in the air means the risk of altitude sickness is increased. Feeling tired after only a little exercise, feeling sick, dizzy or having a headache all point to altitude sickness. Acute altitude sickness can be life-threatening as fluid can build up in the lungs and the brain.

Treatment If sickness is mild, take your time ascending (climb at a rate of approx 300m per day) and your body should acclimatise to the conditions within 1–3 days. Some drugs can help counter the symptoms. If it is acute, descend immediately as this is the only cure, and seek medical attention.

Snowblindness

The cornea of the eye can become burned with exposure to the sun's rays as they reflect off the snow. This results in an incredibly painful condition which feels like there is sand in the eye, often accompanied by a headache and temporary blindness, which can last a few days. If the eyes suffer prolonged exposure to UV rays, there may be permanent loss of vision.

Treatment Prevention is better than cure — wear 99–100% UV protective eye wear. Covering the eyes with cool damp compresses will reduce inflammation and keeping them out of any light will ease pain and speed healing. Symptoms often disappear after 48 hours, much like skin sunburn.

Dehydration

By the time you feel thirsty you are already dehydrated. Your heart rate will increase and you'll feel dizzy, irritable and may have a headache. It's not easy to keep up your water intake when you are frozen to your bones and your cold water bottle is tucked away in your bag. The best solution is to carry a CamelBak, then you can sip away throughout the day.

Treatment Drink plenty of water! And take sports drinks, which will rehydrate you even more quickly. Temporary hospitalisation may be necessary for extreme cases.

Assistance

If you suffer from any of the above injuries you will nearly always require some assistance in getting off the hill – which means that first someone must alert the medical patrol. This can be done by finding a local instructor, ski official or policeman, most of whom have radios, or by sending someone down to the nearest lift station. You'll be removed from the hill in one of the following three ways: On a skidoo, in a 'blood wagon' or in a helicopter. If you are with an injured person on a slope, make sure you can be clearly seen as you wait. If you are below the brow of a hill where slope users may not see you in time to stop, place a warning sign on the brow, such as two crossed skis planted in the snow, or even stand there yourself to warn people. The crossed skis is a universal warning sign for an accident.

Insurance

Most lift pass offices will offer insurance with your pass. Although useful, this will usually only cover any rescue off the mountain. Once you are in hospital, you'll need to foot all your own bills. So it's best to go for insurance that covers all your potential needs. One type of insurance that is common in Europe is Carte Neige. It is inexpensive and can be bought for a season or a day at a time. However, it doesn't cover the potential cost of losing your equipment, twisting your knee and needing physio, or having to fly back a day early or late due to adverse weather conditions.

Insurance seems so unimportant when you don't need it. But when you're facing the prospect of a helicopter rescue bill, a new plane ticket and on-going physio, you suddenly feel you'd sell your best friend for the chance to go back and buy it when you had the opportunity. Don't go anywhere without insurance, preferably the most comprehensive money can buy. The areas specific to skiing and boarding it should cover are:

- ▶ Equipment loss or damage.
- ▶ Loss of other belongings.
- ▶ Accidents on or off-piste/back-country.
- ▶ Accidents on or off the mountain.
- ▶ Illnesses.
- ▶ Cancellations and delays.
- ▶ Lift closures.
- ▶ Other snowsports you may want to take part in, such as heli-skiing, parascending, sledging, etc.

Be sure to check the small print of any insurance document for the activities covered. Although more insurance companies are now happy to cover off-piste boarding and skiing (usually with a guide) as standard, there are still some that will cover skiing and not snowboarding, or will cover on groomed runs but not back-country. As with all insurance, there will be an excess clause. Check how much excess you will be expected to pay if you make a claim (there is no point insuring your equipment for up to £250 if your policy states you are responsible for paying the first £250 of any claim). In most cases you will have to produce a police report if you have had anything stolen. Otherwise the insurance company will not give you a penny.

Some countries have reciprocal healthcare agreements, which means that any emergency operations are free. If you are eligible for this, check that you have all the necessary documentation (eg a signed European Health Insurance Card for EU countries). You may still have to pay for the healthcare at the time, but you can claim it back.

Hire shops will often offer their own insurance for equipment they lend to you. Otherwise check your travel insurance policy to see if you are covered. You will normally have to pay the hire shop initially and then claim the cost back from your insurance company. Make sure you take documented evidence of anything you hope to claim for as insurers can be notoriously slippery when it comes to paying out.

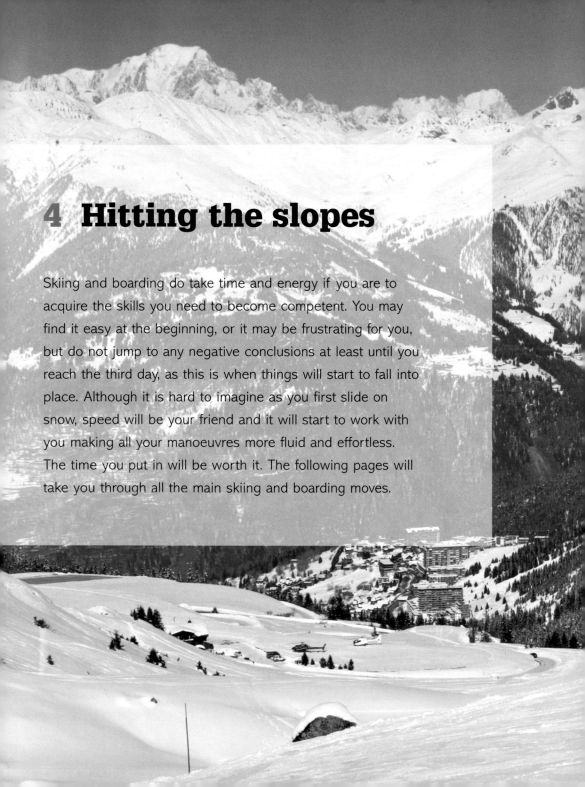

4 Hitting the slopes

Skiing and boarding do take time and energy if you are to acquire the skills you need to become competent. You may find it easy at the beginning, or it may be frustrating for you, but do not jump to any negative conclusions at least until you reach the third day, as this is when things will start to fall into place. Although it is hard to imagine as you first slide on snow, speed will be your friend and it will start to work with you making all your manoeuvres more fluid and effortless. The time you put in will be worth it. The following pages will take you through all the main skiing and boarding moves.

Skiing and snowboarding

There is a very definite series of progressions that have been established for beginners to become proficient in skiing and boarding in the least time possible. Although the progressions evidently have to be different for skiing than for boarding, there are many similarities, this is because, despite the animosity felt between the two sports, they are often identical. Both disciplines require a flexed body which is never static, either extending into a turn or flexing out of a turn. They both use edge pressure in the same way for direction, to traverse, to carve or to stop. Even the turn shapes of a skier and a boarder are now identical, with the introduction of carving and the wide radius turn, and the ability of both boarders and skiers to initiate short-radius turns. The differences between the two are simply down to the direction the body faces and the effect this has on the movements needed to control the skis or board (ignoring the insignificant fact that skiers have poles whereas boarders don't). While a boarder faces sideways, leading with one shoulder and initiating turns partly by leaning with a fore and aft motion, the skier generally faces forwards and initiates turns partly by leaning from side to side.

When it comes to learning the sport, the differences between skiing and boarding stem from the fact that a board has only one edge to balance on, whereas skis have two. It is obviously harder to balance on one edge than two, which means that snowboarders typically fall more and seem to achieve less in the first day or two. However, the learning curve for a boarder is steep, and with confidence a boarder will be solidly proficient after a week. The learning curve for a skier is not so steep as good technique takes slightly longer to master than for a boarder. A skier will still be reasonably proficient after a week, although is unlikely to ski with much style.

Ski etiquette

Skiing is a sport which involves a large number of people flying about in the same area. A 'skiway code' has therefore been developed to try to minimise slope rage and accidents. It's easy to understand and it really does work (unless you are on a beginner slope, where it is every man for himself – enthusiasts are equally as likely to run into you with or without knowledge of the skiway code). The code, as defined by the International Ski Federation (FIS) is as follows:

Rules for skiers

1 **Respect** Do not endanger others.
2 **Control** Adapt the manner and speed of your skiing to your ability and to the general conditions on the mountain.
3 **Choice of route** The skier/snowboarder in front has priority – leave enough space.
4 **Overtaking** Leave plenty of space when overtaking a slower skier/snowboarder.
5 **Entering and starting** Look up and down the mountain each time before starting or entering a marked run.
6 **Stopping** Only stop at the edge of the piste or where you can easily be seen.
7 **Climbing** When climbing up or down, always keep to the side of the piste.
8 **Signs** Obey all signs and markings – they are there for your safety.
9 **Assistance** In an accident, offer help and alert the rescue service.
10 **Identification** All those involved in an accident, including witnesses, should exchange names and addresses.

On the slopes

Erratic behaviour is unhelpful. It is pretty antisocial to change your direction or speed suddenly or extensively, and expect anyone sharing the slope with you to react to what you are doing. Even though theoretically you have right of way if you are below another slope user, s/he is not to know that you are about to suddenly change what you were previously doing.

Skiers and boarders co-exist on the same slopes without injury by understanding a little about each other. Generally skiers are pretty uniform and take short- or medium-radius turns, or a succession of rhythmical longer carved turns. Generally boarders take wider and fewer turns. Boarders need to be given extra room as they have a blind spot on their right side if they ride goofy, or their left if they ride regular. However, both skiers and boarders can change what they are doing at any time, or lose control, so give all slope users room when you pass them.

If you see an accident, or someone lying on a slope, stop and ask if you can help. It may be that they simply need a hand up or help putting a ski back on. If it is more serious, hopefully there will be someone qualified or with a radio (a ski instructor, resort official or medic) near by. If you are a qualified first-aider or have medical training and you can help the injured person, do so. If you are not, the best help you can give is to stay with the person and send someone to the nearest lift station to ask for a medic to be sent out.

Other guidelines to prevent getting shouted at:

In the terrain park:

▶ Do not walk across or on any of the creations in a snow park, including the area used to run up and land. Footprints ruin the smooth snow which has taken someone (usually the park users) a long time to fashion. When the transition on a kicker is uneven it is much harder to control your jump.

▶ Do not cross in front of any park features without checking uphill to see if anyone is just starting their run-up.

▶ Do not cross behind any park feature as it is hard to be seen and you may get landed upon.

▶ Wait your turn when using features in the park.

▶ If a park says 'no skiers' it means no skiers. Skis can ruin painstakingly created features. However, freestyle skis with twin tips are usually allowed as these do not have such a damaging effect.

▶ If you fall, move out of the way as quickly as possible as others will be waiting and they may not see you from above.

▶ Don't walk up the middle of a half-pipe to get to the top. You will get in the way and your footprints create uneven snow.

▶ Be supportive. A park should be a friendly place where all abilities are mixed up together, with the common aim of experiencing that feeling when you go as big as you can and pull off the sweetest trick you can do. Everyone has to start somewhere.

In restaurants:

- ▶ Do de-snow yourself as much as possible before entering to prevent the swimming pool effect.
- ▶ Do leave your skis or board outside and split skis and poles to prevent theft.
- ▶ Do not pick up someone else's skis or board by accident – remember the number on your equipment if it is hired.
- ▶ Don't spend hours in the loo getting out of your ski clothes and holding everyone else up. Take them all off before you go in.

On lifts:

- ▶ Do let ski schools go first.
- ▶ Do sit with people you don't know if that's where you have ended up after queuing, rather than letting empty spaces go while you wait for your buddies.
- ▶ Don't stop the moment you have got off a lift; make sure you are well clear before you stop.
- ▶ Do let snowboarders sit at the sides; it is uncomfortable for a boarder to keep their board straight on a lift as it twists the foot round.
- ▶ Don't think you are hilarious by throwing snowballs at skiers below.
- ▶ Don't worry if the lift stops; this is a frequent occurrence usually caused by high wind or people being a bit slow when getting on or off the lift.

Ski progressions

These progressions take you from never having moved on skis up to carving and freestyle. Although you can move on and forget about most of the manoeuvres once mastered, do not ever forget about your basic stance.

Basic stance

In any sport, there is always a basic stance, which is the best position to be in to perform well. For golf you need straight arms and to be able to bend at the hips; for tennis you need to be flexed, on your toes and rotated as you hit the ball. Skiing is no different. Your basic stance is:

▶ Flexed ankles, knees and hips.
▶ Weight evenly distributed over both feet
▶ ·Feet shoulder-width apart.
▶ Arms away from the body for balance, slightly forward.
▶ Vision at horizon-level, head up.
▶ Upper body facing down the fall line.

Walking Without lifting the ski, shuffle forward and backwards, getting used to the feel of the ski sliding on the snow. Try walking in a large circle, lifting the 'outside' ski to join the 'inside'.

Straight running Find a gradual slope, with a flat run-out area at the bottom. All you need to do is

look up, relax, keep your balance and let your skis run down the hill.
Practice a few times, thinking about all the aspects of the basic stance
and getting used to how it feels to be in the correct position until it
seems perfectly natural.

Main progressions

1 Side stepping On a gradual slope, place your skis across the fall line.
Gripping the snow with the uphill edges of your skis, take a few steps
sideways up the slope, and then back down again.

2 Herringboning This doesn't look very elegant but is the quicker way
of getting up a slope. On a gradual slope, turn your skis until they are

facing uphill, holding a 'V' position and gripping the snow with your inside edges. Keeping the 'V' as wide as possible and making sure the tails of your skis do not cross, step up the hill, pushing outwards rather than upwards and using your poles for balance.

3 **Snow plough** Push the skis out at the same time as your rotate your legs, so that the ski tips point slightly inwards at each other, forming a slight upside down 'V'. Practice holding this position for a little longer each time, and widening the 'V', without slowing the skis down. The snow plough can be used to stop forward movement completely, or simply to brake, by applying more pressure to the inside of your ski.

4 **Plough turns** Turns are something you will need to learn as you will rarely be travelling straight down a slope. To control your speed you will make consistent 's' shaped turns as you travel down the slope. To achieve a plough turn, first practice directing your gliding snow plough off its course: facing down the hill in a slow plough, rotate your left foot inwards so that the tip of your ski points further to the right and you start to move to the right. Then try the same thing with your right foot, so that you start to move to the left. Remember to keep your vision at horizon level.

5 **Plough parallel turns** Initiate a moderate-speed turn with a small plough, placing sufficient pressure on the outside ski to enable the inside ski to level out. As you start to come out of the turn, rotate the

inside leg so that it ceases to point at its partner, but comes round parallel and faces the same direction as the other ski. Try not to lift the inside ski off the snow, rather pivot it under the foot, making sure the skis do not end up close together as you do so.

6   **Parallel turns** The parallel turn has the same components as the plough parallel, but it is a reduction of the movements involved; both skis turn together with no plough initiation. Concentrate on rotating the inner ski earlier and earlier during the turn. Think of steering the turn with both the outer and inner ski, leaning both legs into the turn. Try to unweight your skis when changing edge and flexing down to finish each turn.

7   **Carved traverse** Carving is when you travel on the edge of you skis in the same direction as they are pointing, leaving two thin lines in the snow behind you rather than a broad 'skidded' line. Do not rotate your feet, simply role your ankles so that the skis are on an edge and traveling in a straight line. To carve a traverse, pick up some speed and lean into the hill, pressuring your skis.

8   **Carved turn** This is an extension of the carved traverse but the skis will point down the fall line. Rotate your ankles and then knees towards the slope to bring both skis on to the same edge.

9   **Schussing** The Schuss is simply pointing your skis straight down the slope, maintaining your basic stance. To minimise wind resistence and to rest your torso form a tucked position. Keep your poles parallel to the ground and your feet wider than your shoulder width for balance.

Board progressions

These progressions, although similar to hard-boot progressions, are for a soft-boot set-up with a freestyle/freeride board. If you want to learn on a slalom board instead, the following progressions will help you with general theory but you will need to hire an instructor for more specific guidance.

Basic stance

Achieving the correct basic stance will ensure you not only look good but can ride any type of slope. You may be able to go fast on a groomed slope with a different stance but you will come unstuck on anything more challenging. Your snowboarding basic stance is:

▶ Flexed ankles.
▶ Flexed knees.
▶ Weight evenly distributed over both feet.
▶ Hands out over the nose and tail of the board.
▶ Straight back, head facing direction of travel.
▶ Vision at horizon-level.

Main progressions

1 **Walking** With only your front foot strapped in, find a flat area and walk with the nose of the board facing the way you are going. Then try it with your foot on the other side of the board.

2 **Skating** When you have got your balance, try 'skating' by pushing off from your back foot and then resting it on the board in front of the back binding. Your momentum will keep the board moving for a couple of seconds.

3 **Straight running** On a gentle, gradual slope with a flat area at the bottom, face the nose of the board down the hill and place your back foot on the board in front of your back binding). Looking in the direction of travel with your chin on your shoulder and your hands out over the nose and tail, let the board ride down the slope and stop on the flat.

4a Side slipping On a steeper gradual slope, put your board across the fall line and strap both feet in. To stop moving you will have to lift your toes so that you create an edge and your heels are dug into the snow. Keeping your eyes up, slowly start to drop your toes to begin sliding. To stop, flex down and lift your toes again to create the edge angle, digging your heel edge into the snow. Never let your downhill edge (in this instance your toe edge) touch the snow.

b To do the same thing but on your toe edge, you must roll over so that you are looking up the mountain rather than down. Sit on your bum with your hands away from the snow. Lift both your feet up at the same time as you roll your body across the slope, throwing your board nose over tail or vice versa.

c Side slipping on your toe edge (looking up the hill) is actually easier than on your heels as to create the edge angle all you have to do is flex your knees. Make sure you look up.

5. Falling leaf Start side slipping on your toes or heels until you have a

bit of speed and are balanced. Then put your chin on your
right shoulder and pressure on your right foot. If you
look to your right, downhill slightly, pointing in
the direction of your gaze, you will gradually drift to
the right. To stop, bring your weight back to the centre again
and flex down. By repeating this exercise you will side slip from side to
side of the slope as a leaf falls from a tree – hence the name. The most
important thing is that you look in the direction you want to go.

6   **Garland** The aim here is to pressure the nose of the
board so that it points further and further down the
hill, and then bring it safely across the fall line again
to slow down. Use all the same key skills as in the
above progressions: look in the direction you want to
go; pressure your front foot with a 'pedalling' action; and
flex down with your weight central to stop when the board
is back across the fall line.

7 **The skidded turn** A turn is simply two garlands put together, with a change of edge in between. In other words, your board goes from one edge, to pointing down the hill, then onto the opposite edge to complete the turn. Start directing the board down the hill by pressuring your front foot, and by looking where you want to go and pointing. When the board is in the fall line, keep your balance and slowly continue to look round. The board will follow your vision, at which point you will come up onto the opposite edge by pedalling the back foot either from heel to toe (toe turn) or toe to heel (heel turn). Complete the turn by bringing the board across the fall line and flexing down with your weight distributed evenly over both feet.

Things to remember:

▶ *Keep your hands out over the nose and the tail. Do not let your back hand drift out to the side or it will be harder to direct the board.*

▶ *Keep your weight on your front foot, even though you will be nervous in the fall line. The body's natural reaction to going somewhere too fast is to lean in the opposite direction. This will make you lose control of the board and you'll simply go even faster. Keeping the pressure on your front foot, even though your head is telling you to lean back, will allow you to guide the board out of the fall line. Look where you want to go and not down at the snow or you will fall.*

▶ *Do not try to come up onto your opposite edge too quickly in the middle of the turn. You have to spend some time in the fall line, allowing your board to slowly follow the lead of your vision and your pointing hand. If you try to come up onto the opposite edge while still in the fall line you will fall.*

▶ *Have a laugh. You're sure to end up upside down at some point unless you are unusually gifted. If you're not spending 80% of your time smiling then aren't you wasting valuable time in your short life?*

8   **Linked turns** Once you have nearly completed a turn, without allowing
the board to lose too much speed, begin your next turn. Concentrate
on extending to unweight the board as you initiate the turn, and flexing
to complete the turn. You should never be static but be either slowly
extending or slowly flexing.

9   **Carved traverse** Carving is when you use the rail (edge) of the board
only and travel in the same direction as your board is pointing, rather
than skidding. Edge angle and pressure combine to allow the board to
remain on its edge, so you need some speed. Pick a reasonably steep
slope and traverse across in an arc shape, digging the uphill edge into
the snow by flexing down. Try to feel the support of the edge and let
the sidecut of your board determine the shape of the arc (you cannot
direct the board in a different shape without skidding slightly).

10 **Carved turn** The carved turn differs from the skidded turn because
of the point at which you change edge. Whereas in the skidded turn
you change your edge in the middle of the turn when the board is
facing down the fall line, in the carved turn you change edge earlier
and bring the board round into the fall line and out again with a carved
arc. Cross-over turns are used for large-radius turns where the body
crosses over the board to change edges. Cross under-turns, where the
board crosses under the body while the latter remains perpendicular to
the slope, are used for short-radius carved turns.

Freestyle

Freestyle is the term given to the flashiest aspect of snowboarding and skiing: tricks. Freestyle does not always mean jumping; some tricks are done without you being in the air – in other words you can look good with little effort! You may not want to learn any 'jibbing' manoeuvres or tricks, or your instructor may not consider it an appropriate time to teach them, so you shouldn't assume that you will learn any freestyle in your lessons. However, freestyle (literally 'free' – do as you want – 'style') incorporates such a broad range of tricks, from a simple 'wheelie' to a big air 720° spin, that you sure to pick up some of them. Always hire an instructor and accept that you are unlikely to be able to do many of the tricks you hear about, at least to start with.

Ski freestyle – flatland

To perform ski tricks, you can hold both poles in one hand as opposed to one in each, as they are rarely used. Flatland tricks are just that – tricks on flat land for which you usually do not have to be airborne.

1   **360° Flatland spin** As you complete a short turn keep pressure on the front of your skis until they are pointing up the hill. Once you have almost lost momentum, lean on the backs of your skis and place your weight on the opposite foot, allowing the skis to slide backwards and turning them to form another short turn backwards.

2   **Half cab** Skiing fakie, rotate 180° to forward. Look over your shoulder in the direction you wish to spin and spin with a slight jump so that you have a bit of air.

3   **Nose press/manual** Keeping your weight as far forward as possible, lift the tails of the skis and continue to balance as you slide sideways.

Board freestyle – flatland

1. **360° Flatland spin** Start with a skidded 'U'-shaped turn. As the board is coming to a stop, look over your opposite shoulder and pressure your back foot. Lean down the hill with the opposite foot leading and change onto the opposite edge, forming another 'U'-shaped turn. Repeat.

2. **Wheelie** You will need a flexible board. Practise bouncing onto the nose and tail of your board on a flat area. On a gentle slope, point the board into the fall line and balance on your tail as you are moving. Do not rest on your back foot but lean as if you are trying to tip your board up completely.

3. **Nose and tail roll** Easiest to learn on the completion of a turn. As you are coming to a stop, bring all your weight over your front foot and pull up your back foot as if you are doing a reverse wheelie. Continue rotating your body in the direction of the turn, balancing on your front foot, so that your back foot swings round in the air and down onto the opposite edge.

4. **Ollie and Nollie** An ollie (or nollie if popping off your nose) is the only way to get air when there is no lip or drop to lift you. The idea of an ollie comes from skating and the manoeuvre looks almost the same: the front of the board lifts first, then the back, with the board ending up horizontal in the air before landing with both feet together. Flex down and put your weight on your front foot. Jump up off your back foot and pull your front foot up first, snapping up your back foot and sucking both your knees up underneath you. Stomp down the landing with both feet at the same time.

Park life

....

Snow parks are purpose-built areas specifically for tricks. Usually there will be some kickers (purpose-built jumps); a half-pipe, (a U-shaped design of which both edges are used to jump off, landing back on the same wall each time); and some rails of varying shape to slide along. Every park is different and restricted only by the imagination of the creator.

Pipe The key is not to jump against the wall of the pipe to try to get out of it, but to relax into the pipe and allow the shape of it to gently lift you out as you turn. Start by working on unweighting the skis/board when you loose momentum at the top of the wall. Flex in the pipe and extend as you loose momentum. As you pick up confidence and speed, work at getting to the top and then out of the top of the pipe.

Once you are gently being lifted out of the pipe and getting air, add in some tricks like grabs or rotations (see below).

Rails These do hurt when you fall, make no mistake! So wear protection. Rails are a bit of a gimmick and shouldn't by rights be in a mountain environment, but why let skaters have all the fun? Grinding rails is not easy as you must get your balance right, with the rail exactly underneath your centre of weight.

Boarders – first try a 50/50 by riding along the rail with your board facing the direction of travel. All you have to do is approach it with your board flat, keep your balance and ride it. Next try a board slide on your heel side. A small ollie will get you in position. Make sure your weight is even over both feet, and the rail is right in the middle of your feet. You will naturally lean back, so to compensate throw your arms forward in front of you. Now try toe side board slides by putting your board perpendicular to the length of the rail.

Skiers – approach with enough speed to keep you moving on the rail and split your feet wide for balance when you jump on to it. You do not have the choice of whether to ski straight along it or 50/50 but there are a variety of tricks you can do on and off it such as tail slides etc.

Air

....

When hitting a kicker or riding off a drop, first make sure it is safe.
This means not too big for you, with a surface that's not icy or irregular,
a landing that's steep and long enough (the landing should never be
flat) and with no-one and nothing in your path.

   Ride up to the kicker/drop straight with pressure equally over both
feet, making sure you are not on an edge. Flex on the transition, extend
as you hit the lip and flex on landing, with both feet together.

Grabs Adding grabs to air time both looks good and helps balance you in
the air. There are lots of different grabs, going by a variety of names.

▶ **Ski grabs**

   Mute This is one of the first grabs you'll learn. Suck your knees up to
   your chest and put your hand across in front of you to grab the
   outside edge of the opposite ski.

Japan Underneath the same leg as the hand you are grabbing with, grab the opposite ski.

Safety Grab the outside edge of the same ski as the hand you are grabbing with.

Toxic Grab the inside edge of the same ski.

True tail Reach back and grab the tail of the same ski as the hand you are grabbing with.

▶ **Board grabs** The standard board grabs are:

Indie Your front hand between your bindings on your toe side.

Mute Your back hand between your bindings on your toe side.

Nose Your front hand on the nose.

Tail Your back hand on the tail.

Stalefish Your back hand between your bindings on your heel side.

Method As Stalefish but with an arched back.

Melon Your front hand between your legs on your heel edge.

For all the above, if you add a straightened leg it is known as a 'boned' or 'poked' grab, and if you add two straightened legs it is a 'stiffy'. If you also have your upper body rotating in the opposite direction the grab is known as a 'shifty' air.

Rotating As with all manoeuvres in snowboarding and skiing, rotating demands that you lead with your vision and spot your landing as early as possible. If you are going for a big spin (360˚ or more), counter-rotate before you take off to enable you to get the spin momentum when you are in the air.

Some of the main spins are:

▶ Frontside (rotating clockwise if you are goofy, anti-clockwise if you are regular).

▶ Backside (the opposite).

▶ Anything from 180˚ up to 1080˚ (ie 3 complete rotations) or more, on a straight or leaning axis (eg alley oop or redeo).

Freestyle is an ever-developing discipline and, not surprisingly, the related terminology evolves just as fast. The moves described above are a selection of tricks with common names, however there are hundreds of variations. The roll-call of names can border on the bizarre: Bonk, Burger Flip, Caballerial or Cab, Chicken Salad, Corkscrew, Crail, Crippler, Crossbone Method, Crooked Cop Air, Egg Flip, Eggplant, Flying Squirrel, Fresh Fish, Gay Twist, Haakon Flip, Iguana Air, J-Tear, Jadeo, Japan Air, Lien Air, McEgg, McTwist, Melonchollie Air, Method Air, Miller Flip, Misty Flip, Mosquito, Nuclear, Palmer Air, Phillips 66, Pop Tart, Revert, Rewind, Roast Beef, Rocket, Rodeo Flip, Sad Plant, Seatbelt, Spaghetti, Stalefish, Stalemasky, Suitcase, Swiss Cheese, Tail Slide, and Taipan to name but a few.

In reality most people past about the age of 14 have no idea what each name actually means and still fewer can perform any of these tricks so don't let the plethora of ridiculous names put you off at least trying some freestyle moves!

A note on bumps

Bumps (or Moguls) are special. And not always in a good way. The main thing to remember with bumps is that you need to be much more flexed, with a lower centre of gravity. There are two ways of navigating down a bumps field:

1   Using the rut lines to help you turn around each bump, while gripping the under side of each bump to control your speed.
2   Picking a direct line and minimising your turns and turning movements, so controlling your speed by checking against the top side of each bump where the better snow often is.

Bumps demand different types of edge changes to those described in the previous section, where the torso crosses over the legs ('cross-over' turn) and the edges are changed midway through the turn. Although this method can be used when going slowly around each bump (method 1. above), turning fast on bumps in a direct line will often be achieved by

'sucking up' the legs extensively to absorb the bump, and changing edge
on top of the bump. This is the 'cross-under' method of turning, where
the legs cross under the torso.

For skiing, keep the shoulders pointing down the hill and fix your eyes
on a point at the bottom of the hill. This will allow you to stick to your
chosen line. You will need a more narrow stance to fit through the bumps
and your pole plant will need to be further forward (where third gear
would be found on a car gear stick) in order to keep your weight from
shifting back and to keep the bumps from spitting you out like a dummy.
You need fast hands and fast feet to stay in a line of direct descent on
even a gentle slope.

Most boarders steer clear of bumps but they can be good fun if they
aren't too icy. Although the best technique you can use is to keep the body
relatively in line with the board, with little counter-rotation of the upper and
lower body, this is pretty hard and at high speeds not always possible (the

upper body will anticipate and lead the turn, the lower body will be slower to catch up). Counter-rotation with your upper body will enable you to change edges much more quickly, although it is not as stable a position to maintain and you are more likely to come unstuck if anything forces you off-balance than if you had your upper and lower body in line. As with skiing, pick your line and try to stick to it by focusing on a point at the bottom of the hill.

A note on powder

Powder is loads of fun both on a board and on skis. Pick steep powder fields only, as a gentle gradient will bring you to a frustrating stop and you may be unable to get on top of the snow to get started again. Make sure you lean slightly back and keep your speed up, always keeping the nose of your skis/board out of the snow. Short-radius turns are difficult but sometimes necessary to keep speed in check. Turns will be much like those on groomed snow, except for the pressure on turn initiation. Whereas on groomed snow pressure is applied at the start of a turn, on powder you will not skid, so you do not want to pressure heavily at turn initiation, rather your aim is to keep the skis/board as light as possible and pressure only at the end of the turn.

A note on steeps

Only consider steeps if you are good at short-radius turns and can hold your basic stance throughout, as short turns are the only way you can diffuse the speed build-up. To keep your tail(s) clear of the snow on each turn, extend perpendicular to the slope rather than upwards. For skiers, plant your pole early in the turn and as far down the hill below you as is comfortable.

A note on varied terrain

With varied terrain you never know what you will be hitting, so maintain and exaggerate your basic stance. Flex that bit more and stay relaxed, with muscles ready for anything that may be thrown at you.

A note on lifts

Surface/drag lifts

Most surface lifts are a literally a pain in the backside, or thigh if you're a boarder. Main types are:

▶ Platter or moving/magic carpet.
▶ Button or poma.
▶ J-bar or T-bar.
▶ Crazy rope tows (mainly found in New Zealand, where getting up the hill is made the main sport of the day).

Moving carpets are relatively straightforward and are not painful for skiers or boarders, but **rope tows** are seriously hard work for skier and boarder alike. The rest of the surface lifts, designed for skiers and potentially enjoyable for them, are a nightmare for boarders as the front foot has to twist so that it faces forwards.

Preparation In some countries boarders must take their back foot out of the binding and place it against the back binding on the stomp pad. In other countries it must be strapped in.

No doubt the lifties will shout at you if you're doing it wrong. Skiers must take their hands out of their straps and hold both poles with one hand. Make sure your board/skis are straight before grabbing the bar. Place your weight back slightly, to prepare you for the initial pull.

During These lifts will not support your weight so don't sit down. The idea is to maintain a flexed, basic stance position with your head up, and allow the lift to pull you up the hill (just as if you were being pulled by someone's hand). Skiers need do no more than relax and enjoy the scenery. Boarders must let go of the lift with the back hand and place it out behind for balance (holding with two hands results in the upper body facing forward, which brings the board round with it, so making it hard to keep the board facing the direction of travel).

Boarders on a J or T-bar can place the bar behind both legs but this is uncomfortable and makes it harder to maintain a sideways stance. Placing it behind your front leg is better though not much more comfortable!

Finish There'll be signs to tell you when you are at the end, and you will arrive at a gradual slope which runs off to the side. When you are clearly on the downward slope, unhook the lift and ski off to the side, leaving plenty of room for the next person to get off after you.

Chair lifts

Preparation Boarders should take the back foot out; skiers should hold both poles with one hand. Ensure there's nothing loose about you that is likely to drop from the chair. When in position, with your board/skis facing directly forward, turn your head to watch the chair coming behind you and put down a hand to prevent the chair from banging into your legs.

During Just remember to put down the bar.

Finish There'll be signs to tell you when you're at the end. Lift up the bar when instructed and lift the tips of your skis/board. Point your board forward instead of letting it hang out to one side. Push off from the lift on the downward slope and move far away to avoid getting clonked by the chair as it continues on its way round the corner. Boarders should avoid looking at their feet and should stop with a J-turn, keeping the back foot placed firmly up against the back binding.

5 Weather & terrain

Skiing and snowboarding are extreme sports, affected by varying weather and snow conditions. Although on groomed runs conditions are rarely life-threatening (pisted areas are well maintained and relatively safe from the risk of an avalanche), weather and snow conditions can vary considerably and you may find that the elements push you out of your comfort zone. The ski environment is one of great contrasts. Conditions vary not just from country to country but from slope to slope. Conditions can also vary from one hour to the next and between the top of the run and the bottom. So don't get caught on a blizzard afternoon without your goggles because you've been lulled into a false sense of security by a beautiful sunny morning, or forget your sunnies because you were in cloud in the valley when there's bright sunshine at the top of the mountain.

Weather conditions

Before you set out for the slopes each day, check the weather report for your mountain. This report can be obtained from the local ski patrol or will often be displayed in resort – even in your chalet/hotel if you have travelled with a tour operating company. If there are severe weather conditions, some lifts may be closed so check the lift reports at the base lift station.

Weather lowdown

Sun Good for visibility, bad for sunburn and melting the snow to 'slush'.

Snow Good for 'powder' snow, bad for visibility and getting wet and cold.

Wind Good for creating beautiful snowscapes, bad for lift closure, creating solid, icy slopes and wind-chill which reduces the body's temperature.

Rain Bad all round. Turns the snow to very sticky slush which is impossible to ski/ride on. Makes for very miserable, cold and wet skiers and boarders. (Luckily it doesn't rain too often on the slopes but it's something to look out for on the lower resorts as the world gets warmer.)

Cloud Bad for visibility as cloud creates 'flat' light. This means that there are no shadows to show up contours in terrain. Good if it brings snow along with it!

Snow conditions

Whereas weather conditions affect the quality of your skiing by affecting your general enjoyment and confidence, snow conditions affect your general enjoyment and confidence by affecting the quality of your skiing. Different snow conditions are beneficial for different aspects of skiing, for example powder is great for wide carved turns but useless for a beginner learning a skidded turn. Each resort is likely to have different snow conditions on different runs, depending on, for example, which way the slope is facing, or how many people use it.

► **Fresh groomed snow** A 'corduroy' piste with soft snow is ideal for boarders and skiers. This snow condition occurs after the grooming machines (piste bashers/bullies) have been out and evened out the snow with a big comb.

► **Icy snow** Common in March and April or on glaciers in the summer when the snow melts in the afternoon and freezes to hard smooth ice in the morning, or in resorts affected by wind where fresh snow is blown away. Avoid icy snow wherever possible as it is hard to get an edge and control the board/skis. If you find yourself on ice, do not try to brake, just flatten your board/skis and stop or turn when you are on good snow again.

► **Slush** Common on glaciers in the summer or on afternoons in March and April when the hot sun melts the snow. This is not too bad for boarders, as the board cuts straight through the mounds that are formed, but is unbalancing and frustrating for skiers. It is harder work on the legs for skier and boarder alike.

► **Powder** Regarded by many as the ultimate snow condition as it feels like floating on air – and doesn't hurt if you fall! However, it can be both dangerous and frustrating to get stuck in powder and skiing in the stuff demands a different technique from piste skiing or boarding. Taking on a powder field is not to be done lightly. It is vital that the slope is steep in order to keep momentum - but if off-piste beware of the avalanche risk (see page 105).

► **Varied terrain** Off-piste tends to throw up a variety of snow conditions. One minute you may be hitting ice, if the slope faces the sun, next minute you'll be in deep powder. Off-piste demands a relatively high level of skill to accommodate these varying conditions, and extra attention should be paid to flexion so that the body is able to absorb whatever is thrown at it.

Check the avalanche risk rating at the main lift station. Avalanches can occur on marked runs so the avalanche risk report is not just for those going on back-country missions.

Terrain on- and off-piste

On-piste

On groomed runs the terrain is not particularly hazardous but is still variable enough to be interesting. The aim of any resort is to present its skiers with well-marked and well-maintained runs with uniform snow conditions (ie even, corduroy snow cover). Although different runs will throw up different terrain, any potentially disastrous areas will be marked, such as cliff faces or rocks and boulders. However, you should keep it in mind that snow conditions can change a slope from a uniform powder field to an icy mogul field in a couple of days, or convert a harmless beginner run into an impossible ice rink (and a happy beginner skier into a highly frustrated one) without warning.

For challenging terrain, find the steeps that your resort has to offer, the snow park, or any permanent or temporary mogul fields.

Back-country/off-piste

Following the lead of radical snowboarders, skiing outside the controlled conditions of groomed runs is now standard for the intermediate and advanced. In the US and Canada there are controlled zones which, although un-groomed, are deemed safe to explore. However, in Europe you really are on your own, with resort officials leaving you in the hands of any avalanche threat you may encounter. Of course they will kindly come and try to dig you out in time should you bury yourself in an avalanche (90% of fatal avalanches are set off by those they kill), but they will not render off-piste areas safe from avalanches as the Americans do. So if you do venture off the marked runs, take a local qualified mountain guide and learn about avalanches and what equipment to take with you beforehand. If you go when the conditions are right, you will undoubtedly have the

most awesome and beautiful experiences that it is possible to have in the sport, with fresh tracks and incredible snowscapes.

Hazardous back-country conditions Escaping the watchful eye of resort officials (especially from the 'speed check police' in some resorts) and getting away from the crowds is certainly tempting, but it does bring its hazards. Going off-piste entirely on your own is foolish. If you have a fall and can't find a ski, hit your head or twist something, a normally non-threatening situation suddenly becomes life-threatening. Your mobile phone may have the latest in video and internet technology but if it can't find a signal it's about as much use to you as sign language to a blind man.

Getting lost is more of a pain in the neck than a hazard, but it means you'll end up on flat land having to spend hours walking through deep snow to get to where you wanted. It is very irritating and extremely hard work if you have to waste a beautiful afternoon hiking out of somewhere you didn't mean to be in the first place. In addition, you may find you are still hiking when it gets dark; spending the night in freezing conditions, unprepared, is obviously a fantastically bad idea.

Check your insurance small print as some insurance companies will not insure you if you are off the groomed runs.

Avalanches

Although groomed runs are protected by control methods such as blasting susceptible areas with dynamite, or avalanche barriers above treelines, avalanches can still occur on-piste (although they are highly unlikely), and often do off-piste. There are an estimated 100,000 avalanches every year (most unwitnessed). Avalanches are categorised as loose snow, wet snow or slab avalanches, all of which result from the instability of the snowpack. If there is little cohesion between layers of snow, or between the snow and the ground, then, dependent on other factors, there may be an avalanche.

Essentially avalanches occur because of the relationship between the terrain, weather, snowpack and specific events:

► **Terrain** While avalanches can occur on slopes of between 15° and 60°, they are more likely to occur between the gradients of 30° and 45°. Convex slopes create stresses and fracture lines and, especially when a convex area is high up on the slope, are more likely to create an avalanche. Trees reduce the pressure of the snow by breaking up the total mass and holding sections of the slope firm.
► **Weather** Determines how the snowpack has formed over time and how stable the snowpack is.
► **Snowpack** A solid snowpack of cohesive snow means no avalanche.
► **Specific events** Among the events that trigger avalanches are a ski-pole planting on a weak fracture point, a cornice or ice falling, or dynamite exploding (controlled avalanches).

6 Where to go

The popularity of skiing has created accessible and well-maintained resorts the world over, giving a great choice for skiers and boarders of all abilities and ages. You can ski in Andorra, Argentina, Australia or Austria through to Scotland, Serbia, Slovenia, Spain, Sweden, Switzerland and, last but not least, the United States. If it has a mountain high enough you can probably find a tour operator that'll take you there. Although it's assumed that choice is always desirable, in fact the more choice there is, the harder it is to make a decision and the more time wasted agonising over where to go. There are thousands of resorts, each purporting to be better than the other. Don't stress; if there is snow, you will have fun, and most resorts will have snow unless you are unlucky. Use this chapter to help you choose.

VETEMENTS
DE SPORTS

Ski area

Nearly every resort publishes a ski map showing lifts, runs, restaurants and altitude of the resort. These are easy to get hold of and are a great help in deciding where to go. The factors influencing your decision will be: the altitude, lifts, runs and direction of slope faces (the aspect).

Altitude

Unfortunately, due to rising temperatures perhaps attributable to global warming, snow cover in many resorts is less than certain. This is becoming the main factor in deciding where to go skiing and will continue to be so if temperatures carry on rising as predicted. Higher resorts will usually have a more lengthy season and better snow (although those resorts above the treeline can be very windy and avalanche-prone without trees to anchor the snow).

Although Canada, like the UK, has adopted the metric system in everyday life, in skiing (for some reason known only to them) they follow the Americans and have their measurements in feet. To complicate matters further, Americans have two different measurements for a foot; the old measurement which bore no relevance to the rest of the world's foot, and the updated version, which thankfully is the same as everyone else's. The measurements normally used are:

1 foot	=	**0.3048 metres**
1 metre	=	**3.28083989 feet**

If you are going mid-season, look for the skiable area of a resort to start around 1,000m/3,280ft and the top of the resort to be upwards of 2,000m/6,560ft. If you are going early or late in the season the height of the resort is even more important. Low resorts such as those in the Pyrenees may have their season shortened by 20% within the next 30–40 years and are already suffering from a thinner base of snow. If you are going early or late, look for a resort located as high as possible, at least 1,500m/4,920ft and preferably above 1,800m/5,900ft. This does not guarantee snow cover at the beginning of the season, as the altitude of a land mass bears little relevance to the weather conditions on any particular day. It does, however, affect the temperature, which gives any wet conditions the best chance to turn to snow and stay frozen on the ground. It is not so important for your accommodation to be high, as long as you don't mind traveling up to the snow in a cable car or bus.

Lifts

Note The lift and runs information may not be helpful to Nordic skiers, who should check resort websites for Nordic trail guidelines.

Beginner boarders Look for a resort with chair lifts and cable cars rather than drag lifts. Drag lifts (see page 95) are a pain on a board as you have to keep your foot twisted all the way up while keeping your balance, added to which all the stress of the pull up goes onto one leg only. If possible, choose an area with a beginner slope served by a chair lift.

Beginner skiers Look for an area with at least three of any type of lift serving green or blue runs.

Intermediate and advanced skiers and boarders Look for an area with enough diversity to keep you interested (five lifts serving different slopes would be a minimum to keep your interest for a week).

Freestyle skiers and boarders Look for a terrain park with a lift if you want a busy park with spectators, or without if you want serious freestylers. Note that some maps show kiddies' play areas as 'snow parks' whereas others call terrain parks 'snow parks'. Check with the resort each year for specific features, as parks are not always created exactly as advertised.

Runs

If you're thinking of skiing on the other side of the Atlantic, note that 'skiable area' has different meanings on different sides of the pond. Also, while Americans often define their skiable area in acres, Europeans will tend to refer to kilometres of runs. And both sides of the pond will find some way to prove that their runs are the biggest. Comparisons can be made but take each published statistic and related statement of quality with a pinch of salt.

Runs are colour graded with the skier in mind, using steepness as the measure. The steeper the slope or any sections of the slope, the higher the grading. This means that you won't encounter even a small section of steep slope on a green run. Bumps or Mogul fields are also added into the equation, as a run with bumps is harder work than the same gradient slope without bumps.

Being the newcomers to the sport, boarders are not included in this grading system. Boarders find steeper runs easier, as they can side slip (see page 82), but a green run with flat bits is impossible as beginner boarders cannot go straight very easily, nor can they keep up momentum and will probably have to take their board off and walk. It pays for a boarder to have a little local knowledge as a map is unlikely to show flat areas or narrow paths on a run.

Colour grading for runs

Difficulty	Europe	America
Beginner	Green	Green
Beginner/intermediate	Blue	Blue
Intermediate/advanced	Red	Black diamond
Advanced	Black	Double black diamond

Beginner boarders Generally red runs are steeper, which is better for a boarder, but they could still have flat sections in the middle. Look for an area with a beginner slope plus at least five blues and preferably a few reds/black diamonds.

Beginner skiers Look for an area with a beginner slope plus at least five long greens and blues.

Intermediate and advanced skiers and boarders Look for a large skiable area with at least two or three blacks/double black diamonds and a variety of reds/black diamonds. Check if the hill/mountain is linked to any other resorts to extend the skiable area.

Freestylers and freeriders Look for an area with some challenging off-piste (you may need some local knowledge) and a terrain park, preferably with a half-pipe at a reasonable altitude to maintain good snow.

Direction of slope faces

Snow condition depends on which way a slope faces. As a rule mountains in the northern hemisphere tend to have sunny south-facing slopes in the morning with snow melting more quickly than on north-facing slopes, and sunny west-facing slopes in the afternoon when the sun is hotter and melts the snow more quickly. In the southern hemisphere, the east- and west-facing slopes will be the same as in the northern hemisphere, but the north and south will be the opposite. Therefore the south-facing slopes will keep their snow longer but will be in the shade for a greater part of the day than the north-facing slopes.

Mountains face a variety of directions and have no regard for the human need to quantify degrees in a convenient north, south, east, west system. Plus the time of year, gradient of a slope, weather conditions and altitude of surrounding mountains all play a part in determining how much sun a slope will get. If you can obtain local knowledge before you go, you'll be at an advantage. Otherwise, choose a resort where you can ski on both north- and south-facing slopes, so you can choose sunny mornings before the snow gets slushy, then ski over the opposite side in the afternoon as the snow starts to soften.

Other factors

Weather reports

If you have the luxury of waiting till the last minute to book a ski trip, you can base your decision on recent weather reports, including the amount of snow cover. Even if you book early, check the past weather conditions for that area. Bear in mind that perfect snow conditions are not the only ingredient in the perfect skiing experience. If you are a beginner you won't necessarily want to go to an area which is always freezing but with great fresh snow, such as Whistler in Canada in January. You may want sunny days and softer snow on which to learn, for example Pas de la Casa in Andorra in the spring.

Price

If price is a major concern the main variants to consider are the following: lift pass, accommodation, equipment hire, food, transport to and from the resort, children's activities such as crèches, ski school and, finally, après-ski. Prices will obviously be affected by the rise and fall of different currencies, which may influence where you decide to go.

Take into account *all* of the above factors when looking for a cheap deal. If you pick just one of the above prices for comparison, for example accommodation, you may find that the overall cost of your trip is higher than it would be in a place with more expensive accommodation. Often accommodation or transport is subsidised by a tour operator, which makes a week seem cheap, but the cost in resort of food, alcohol or equipment hire may blow your trip's budget.

Kids

Operators and agents are falling over themselves to cater for children, as are resorts, with on-hill crèches and snow play areas, kids' ski schools and nannying services in the evenings. Because of this extensive choice, kids are no longer a major factor in determining where to go. In most places, children from age 5 upwards are able to join ski lessons, with some resorts allowing 4-year-olds to learn to ski. Check minimum ages with the resort in advance.

Accommodation

Although not a direct influence on your skiing experience as far as the sport itself goes, your accommodation will add (or not) to your enjoyment of the trip as a whole. There are three main types of accommodation:

- ▶ Hotel
- ▶ Catered chalet or apartment
- ▶ Self-catered chalet or apartment

Most people of average stamina will be knackered after a day's skiing and will want a meal prepared for them (and won't want to go out to a restaurant every night). This is why catered chalets are the most popular choice. However, as long as you do not have to stick to specific meal times in your hotel (you may be offered night skiing in your resort, or may want to stay for promotional après-ski in a local bar), and provided there are others happy to share the cooking, hotels and self-catered accommodation have plenty to recommend them.

Trekking for miles to get from your accommodation to the slopes is not much fun. If you do choose accommodation which is not near a lift or a slope, check whether there are frequent local buses. Most resorts offer free bus services throughout the day on presentation of your lift pass. Also check if there is anywhere to leave your equipment so that you don't have to carry it backwards and forward every day wearing cumbersome ski boots.

If you choose to stay on the edge of a slope, check whether buses operate in the evenings to take you to local shops, bars and restaurants.

Après-ski

Although skiing and boarding are serious sports, they have become associated with evening leisure activities too. With skiing you cannot walk out of the front door and enjoy the sport for an hour or two, as you would with jogging or tennis, so skiing inevitably becomes a holiday, with all the normal holiday activities that come with it. If you have the energy, resort nightlife can be buzzing every night of the week. Choose a resort with a choice of bars (which includes most resorts in the world) and preferably tour operator presence as this brings with it staff who always want to party!

Other common après-ski activities are swimming, local excursions, bowling and ice-skating, to name a few. On-snow activities include skidooing or snowmobiling (better in America as it is largely banned as a sport in Europe), sledging or tubing, ice or indoor wall climbing, parascending or parapenting and even reindeer sledging in some resorts!

Snow-shoeing is becoming more popular and resorts will often hire equipment and a guide, so those of you partial to a stroll will find more and more resorts will accommodate you.

Special needs

Skiing has come on in leaps and bounds in terms of accommodating those with special needs. Resorts are more accessible, hire shops more in touch with specialist equipment and schools will often have specially trained instructors. Alternatively there are clubs and societies that will tailor-make ski trips from your home country. It is a common occurrence to see someone on a sit-ski flying down a slope or a blind skier skiing with a guide. Nowadays there is little to stop those with special needs from enjoying the sport to the full.

Mountain restaurants

If you are either pretty loaded, or looking for a relaxed trip in which you can eat every day atop a mountain and relax there all afternoon, you should check out how many mountain restaurants your resort offers. If there are only one or two then you will find it quite boring if you have to eat there every day, plus the place may be very crowded around lunch time. Restaurants are usually shown on ski maps. Be aware that prices are understandably hiked up in mountain restaurants as some poor soul has to venture up there with deliveries every week.

International resort guide

Africa

Lesotho
Oxbow
Altitude: 2,600m/8,528ft Lifts: 2
▶ Great for summer snow
▶ Basic facilities

Morocco
Oukaimeden
Altitude: 3,258m/10,689ft Lifts: 8
▶ Donkey rides to surrounding areas

Asia

China
Yabuli Ski Resort
Altitude: 1,256m/4,122ft Lifts: 9
▶ China's premier resort
▶ Night skiing
▶ Has the world's longest toboggan run

India
Gulmarg (Himalayas)
Altitude: 4,138m/1,3576ft Lifts: 6
▶ One of the world's highest skiable areas
▶ Heli-skiing
▶ Budget accommodation

Iran
Dizin
Altitude: 3,500m/11,483ft Lifts: 8

▶ Day lift pass for around £2 ($4)
▶ Purpose-built blocks; un-maintained slopes

Israel
Mount Hermon
Altitude: 2,000m/6,560ft Lifts: 7
▶ Extreme weather conditions
▶ Runs generally un-maintained

Japan
Hukuba Iwatake (Negano)   Altitude: 1,289m/4,229ft Lifts: 15
▶ Snow park
▶ Accessible off-piste

Hirafu (Hokkaido)
Altitude: 1,200m/3,937ft Lifts: 18
▶ Can be difficult to get across the whole skiable area

Korea
Phoenix Park
Altitude: 1,050m/3,444ft Lifts: 9
▶ Snow park with a half-pipe
▶ Can suffer from poor snow conditions

Pakistan
Malam Jabba
Altitude: 2800m/9200ft Lifts: 2
▶ Pakistan's only resort & often closed
▶ Lifts of questionable safety

Australia

New South Wales
Perisher Blue
Altitude: 2,084m/6,837ft Lifts: 45
► Australia's largest skiing area with 4 resorts

Tasmania
Ben Lomond
Altitude: 1,572m/5,156ft   Lifts: 8
► Can suffer poor snow
► Not great for boarders

Victoria
Mt Buller
Altitude: 1,780/5,827ft Lifts: 25
► Fun & friendly
► Well-maintained runs & freestyle facilities

Canada

Alberta
Lake Louise
Altitude: 2,637m/8,652ft Lifts: 11
► Scenic runs
► Well-maintained freestyle structures

British Columbia
Whistler-Blackcomb   Altitude: 2,182m/7,160ft Lifts: 33
► Biggest skiing area in North America
► Affordable & well maintained

New Brunswick
Crabbe Mountain Altitude: 404m/1,325ft Lifts: 4
Mont Farlagne
Altitude: 323m /1,060ft Lifts: 4

Newfoundland
Marble Mountain
Altitude: 498m/1,633ft Lifts: 5
► Good steeps for downhill
► Good flat for cross-country

Nova Scotia
Wentworth
Altitude: 302m/990ft Lifts: 7
► Can be crowded
► Snow cover can be poor but good artificial snow

Ontario
Mount St Louis
Altitude: 396m/1,300ft Lifts: 14
► Great artificial snow
► Very modern lifts

Quebec
Tremblant
Altitude: 914m/3,001ft Lifts: 12
► Among Canada's most popular resorts
► Near-perfect snow at any time of day (4 faces)

Europe

Andorra
Pas de la Casa
Altitude: 2,640m/8,661ft Lifts: 31
► Well-maintained runs & park with snowboard/skier cross course
► Extensive skiing area

Austria
Beautiful Innsbruck City is the gateway to 7 local resorts and home to the International Snowboard Federation, as well as being a resort in its own right.

Neustift and the Stubai glacier
Altitude: 3,200m/10,500ft Lifts: 19
▶ Year-round skiing
▶ Snow park

St Anton
Altitude: 2,811m/9,222ft Lifts: 34
▶ The mother of all ski resorts, steeped in history
▶ Mainly for advanced
▶ Busy & a little pricey

Bulgaria
Borovets
Altitude: 2,530m/8,300ft Lifts: 11
▶ Affordable

England, Ireland and Wales
Sorely behind the rest of Europe in terms of snow-covered mountains but with great dry and artificial snow slope culture.
▶ 2 snow domes, more to come
▶ many dry slopes, nearly all with dedicated training & freestyle evenings

Finland
Levi
Altitude: 725m/2,378ft Lifts: 19
▶ Great for Nordic; average for downhill
▶ 2 half-pipes

France
Les Trois Vallées claims to be the most extensive ski area in the world, with 200 lifts and incorporating Courchevel, La Tania, Meribel, Mottaret, Val Thorens (the highest) and Les Menuires.

Chamonix
Altitude: 3,842m/12,605ft Lifts: 48

▶ Great for extreme sports junkies
▶ Good snow cover & large skiing area

Germany
Garmisch
Altitude: 2,830m/9,285ft Lifts: 38 lifts
▶ Well developed & maintained
▶ Parks, pipes & a glacier

Greece
Mt Parnassos
Altitude: 2,260m/7,415ft Lifts: 16
▶ Greece's main resort
▶ Can be crowded

Greenland
Sisimiut
Altitude: 1600m/5250ft Lifts: 1
▶ Nordic resort
▶ Home to the 'Arctic Circle Race' – an extreme way to spend 3 days

Italy
Courmayeur
Altitude: 2,755m/9,039ft Lifts: 30
▶ Colledel Gegante glacier offers summer & winter skiing
▶ Elegant resort
▶ Good snow cover

Pila
Altitude: 2,750m/9,022ft Lifts: 13
▶ Far more affordable than nearby France
▶ Cable link to Aosta town

Norway
Trysil
Altitude: 1,100m/3,608ft Lifts: 24 (mainly surface)
▶ Norway's largest single resort with

some of best winter skiing on offer
► Perfect snow but bitterly cold

Poland
Zakopane
Altitude: 1,960m/6,430ft   Lifts: 20
► Affordable
► Rich culture

Romania
Poiana Brasov
Altitude: 1,800m/5,905ft   Lifts: 11
► Romania's most well-developed resort
► Centred around a lake

Russian Federation
Cheget
Altitude: 1,340m/4,396ft   Lifts: 5
► Russia's largest resort
► Can be a rather 'raw' experience with poor snow, run & lift maintenance

Scotland
Glenshee
Altitude: 1,060m/3,478ft   Lifts: 26 (24 surface)
► Snow cover can be poor

Slovak Republic Jasna
Altitude: 2,000m/6,560ft   Lifts: 24 (mainly surface)
► Busy around Christmas & Easter

Slovenia
Krvavec
Altitude: 1,970m/6,462ft   Lifts: 13
► Affordable
► Less crowded than other Slovenian resorts
► Snow conditions cannot be guaranteed

Spain
Candanchú
Altitude 2,400m/7,874ft   Lifts: 24
► Affordable
► Little nightlife to speak of

Sweden
Åre
Altitude: 1,420m/4,659ft   Lifts: 44
► Great views of picturesque villages
► Ignored by most foreign tour operators
► Can have long lift queues

Switzerland
Verbier
Altitude: 3,330m/10,925ft   Lifts: 48
► Meet the rich and famous
► Longer season than most resorts
► Glacial skiing

Saas Fee
Altitude: 3,550m/1,1647ft   Lifts: 26
► Relatively untouched, quiet village
► Great off-piste skiing
► Good snow cover

New Zealand
....

North Island
Whakapapa ('Wh' pronounced 'F')
Altitude: 675m/2,214ft   Lifts: 24
► Average snow conditions
► Extensive, varied & accessible off-piste

South Island
Remarkables
Altitude: 325m/1,066ft   Lifts: 5
Coronet Peak
Altitude: 428m/1,404ft   Lifts: 7
► Affordable

▶ Great parks, night skiing & nightlife
▶ Snow cover can be poor

South America

....

Argentina
Las Leñas
Altitude: 3,431m/11,253ft   Lifts: 11
▶ Highest resort in the Andes
▶ Off-piste extensive if wind-blown

Bolivia
Chacaltaya
Altitude: 5,422m/17,785ft   Lifts: 1
▶ Very high so retains snow
▶ Altitude sickness can be a problem

Chile
Valle Nevado
Altitude: 3,659m/12,000ft   Lifts: 9 (links
to La Parva and El Colorado, offering 42
lifts in total)
▶ Part of rapidly developing skiing area
▶ Holds good snow

Venezuela
Mérida
Altitude: 4,765m/15,633ft   Lifts: 1
▶ Lift queues can be up to 4 hours
▶ Cliff drops & crevasses are not for the
  faint-hearted

USA

....

The east side of the US offers a variety
of resorts, most small and purpose-built,
often with more artificial snow than real
stuff. In the western US everything is
generally bigger, apart from the lift
queues. The lack of crowding makes
the wide open slopes seem larger still, and
the food and accommodation has the big
man in mind.

Alaska
Alyeska
Altitude: 1,200m/3,939ft   Lifts: 9
▶ Mainly for intermediate & advanced
▶ Terrain park
▶ Night skiing

Alabama
Cloudmont Ski Resort
Altitude: 548m/1,800ft   Lifts: 2
▶ Poor in terms of altitude & facilities
▶ Somehow survives in balmy Alabama

Arizona
Sunrise Park
Altitude: 3,352m/11,000ft   Lifts: 10
▶ Rising from the desert & run by the
  White Mountain Apache Tribe
▶ Good downhill & cross-country runs

California
Heavenly
Altitude: 3,000m/10,000ft   Lifts: 29
▶ Links with 5 areas around Lake Tahoe
  on a single lift pass
▶ Great views of Lake Tahoe & Nevada
  Desert
▶ Good snow with artificial back-up

Colorado
Aspen
Altitude (Aspen Mountain):
3,815m/12,518ft   Lifts: 39 (over 3 areas,
linked by free bus)
▶ Aspen Mountain for intermediate &
  advanced; Buttermilk for beginners

Breckenridge
Altitude: 3,962m/12,998ft   Lifts: 26
▶ At forefront of drive to lift bans on boarders in Colorado
▶ Extremely cold – you may feel the effects of reduced oxygen
▶ Good access to 5 other areas, including the popular Vail

Connecticut
Powder Ridge
Altitude: 228m/750ft   Lifts: 7
Mount Southington
Altitude: 160m/525ft   Lifts: 7
▶ Good freestyle facilities

Georgia
Sky Valley
Altitude: 1,066m/3,500ft   Lifts: 2
▶ Great family resort, with golf facilities
▶ Limited skiable terrain

Idaho
Sun Valley
Altitude: 2,798m/9,150ft   Lifts: 18
▶ Upmarket, elegant resort with cultured après-ski
▶ Challenging terrain

Illinois
Chestnut Mountain
Altitude: 317m/1,040ft   Lifts: 8
▶ Good park facilities

Indiana
Perfect North
Altitude: 243m/800ft   Lifts: 13
▶ Crowded but more lifts than most midwest resorts

Iowa
Fun Valley
Altitude: 378m/1,240ft   Lifts: 5
▶ Tubes, park & a pipe

Maine
Sunday River
Altitude: 957m/3,140ft   Lifts: 18
▶ Good artificial snow
▶ Great freestyle parks with minipipe for beginners & hits & jibs for advanced

Maryland
Wisp
Altitude: 939m/3,080ft   Lifts: 7
▶ Good park facilities
▶ Overcrowded

Massachusetts
Jiminy Peak
Altitude: 728m/2,390ft   Lifts: 10
▶ Among the largest & highest of Massachusetts' small fields

Michigan
Alpine Valley
Altitude: 369m/1,210ft   Lifts: 20

Montana
Big Mountain
Altitude: 2,133m/7,000ft   Lifts: 10
▶ Fantastic tree-skiing
▶ Consistently good snow

Nevada
Mount Rose
Altitude: 2,960m/9,700ft   Lifts: 7
▶ Extensive terrain parks
▶ Backs onto beautiful Lake Tahoe